Agile Coaching :

Where to Start?

Dmitri Iarandine

Copyright © 2017-2018 Dmitri Iarandine

All rights reserved.

ISBN: 9781976828232

CONTENTS

1	Preface	1
2	Introduction	10
3	Agile Coach vs Scrum Master	21
4	Setting up for Success	26
5	Coaching Journey Outline	31
6	Coaching Framework - Start	40
7	Coaching Framework - Progressing	52
8	Agile Adoption Maturity	68
9	Measuring Agile Adoption	74
10	Coaching Definition of Done	82
11	Conclusion	89
12	About the Author	95

1 PREFACE

Agile Coaching remains a prominent career progression trend for a large percentage of Agile Project Management and Digital Delivery professionals who outgrew the shoes of a Scrum Master.

What we see on the job market and by observing our professional social media feeds, is more and more of our contacts changing their titles to append the trendy "/Agile Coach" suffix to whatever they were called before.

In most of those cases you can say with confidence that the person is stretching into the area that potentially interests them (and often pays more), but likely doesn't have a solid base of knowledge and tools at their disposal that would qualify them as a properly prepared Agile Coach, there to serve a very specific and new organizational purpose.

Even more often, a hypothetical Scrum Master - as the most common candidate for progression into an Agile Coaching role - sees the growing market demand and wonders whether or not they should do the same as many other professionals are doing. But where exactly to start that next leg of their career transitioning journey remains really unclear to most of the professionals I've interviewed.

This book is my attempt to summarize my learnings and observations from inside the Agile professional space, explaining in simple terms what an Agile Coach is really supposed to do, how they are different from Agile Delivery roles such as Scrum Master, and ultimately how to properly transition into the role, becoming useful to your organization and assisting other engaged roles.

Two years of my research and study of Agile Coaching body of knowledge specifically, revealed a bunch of usually disconnected blogs and articles that give you glimpses of Agile Coaching activity, still lacking any sort of consistency, connecting those fragments of information into a logical coaching journey or even a professional Roadmap, fitting into a typical picture of Enterprise-scale transformation.

Is this for Enterprise-scale coaching purposes only then? Not necessarily.

While a lot of what we'll be reviewing and discussing in the chapters of this book will relate closely to larger scale operations, most of coaching concepts, goals and general direction could be applied virtually anywhere - even in Lean Agile startup environments.

There are a few other good books out there that take their own attempts at breaking down what being an Agile Coach really means and how to coach the Teams.

I believe that the key difference of my book is in the angle that I choose to take in this narrative, outlining typical Coaching journey and what you should be focusing on at different stages of it, letting you see the breadth of the matter, rather than its depth. The thing is that when we focus on depth - i.e. implementation and execution of specific methods and practices that should help you coach people, per se - we tunnel vision into the "HOW" inevitably, rather than stay high-level enough to continue seeing the horizon.

The other Agile Coaching books that I had the pleasure of reading focus on Agile Coaching process as the **Destination***. This book looks at Agile Coaching as a* ***Journey*** *of an individual becoming an Agile Coach who needs to see where they are headed.*

What I'd ultimately like to offer you in this book is rather quickly and informally tell you what are the main things you need to know before stepping into an Agile Coaching role, and what you should do on day one, as well as consider doing on day 365.

The content of this book should be also useful to professional Recruiters who assist companies in finding the right personnel filling in Agile job openings, including Agile Coaching roles that we see emerge more frequently among online job ads these days.

Paradox of being a long time in the industry of delivering Web and Digital Online Projects is that you get used to the legacy ways of doing things and how organizations perceive certain roles. So the longer you've been in one of those roles, or perhaps hired professionals to fill those roles, the more used you are to the old ways of measuring organizational suitability of the job candidates.

The most important thing to understand before diving deeper into the topics of the following chapters is that it is not just about sheer volume of extra knowledge that an Agile Coach must possess compared to others.

It is that Agile Coaching approach, goals and methods are very different from what you might be used to as a professional exposed to Agile Project Management, Recruitment or Delivery. This "other side of the same coin" is definitely worth exploring together, and I'm happy to offer you as much information as I've managed to gather and collate over the years.

I sincerely hope that you'll enjoy reading this book, and that you'll learn something new - be it the coaching methods or tools you've never heard of, or soft-skill angles to look out for, while developing your own ways to establish the Learning and Continuous Improvement culture for the good of your organization.

What this book covers?

For those of you who like bullet points and don't have much time - even when reading a book - let me give you a quick rundown of main topics covered in each chapter.

Introduction should serve as the starting point, where I'll try and set the scene for you, talking about Agile Coaching as one of destinations of a career journey that we as individuals might choose to take, pursuing our own professional goals that align with our personal values.

I encourage you not to skip the Introduction, as it's designed to help align your expectations as a reader, sharing insight into how I became an Agile Coach myself and what approach I believe in.

Chapter 1 will shed some light on the high-level Agile Coaching approach, understanding which would help guide you through the rest of the material in this book.

Among other things, we will define Agile Coaching role and purpose here, comparing it to that of a Agile/Scrum Trainer and a Scrum Master as two most commonly known and mistakenly perceived as a replacement for a full time Agile Coach.

Chapter 2 will talk about what criteria should be ideally satisfied to make sure you can succeed as an Agile Coach attempting to transform an organization, or effectively take part in such transformation.

It also tells you as a hiring professional or a Senior Manager about how to set your Coach for success, and make sure they are most efficient in their ability to influence positive change of your company.

Chapter 3 expands on the Coaching Approach and creates a typical outline for a Coaching Journey within a hypothetical organization.

I will review main phases and sub-phases of this journey, briefly describing what you should expect to happen during those, and how your own involvement as an Agile Coach would change over time.

Chapter 4 starts looking at Coaching Services you should consider providing to your teams to create positive momentum aligned with overall Agile Transformation that your company is undergoing.

During the course of this book you will hear me use terms like Coaching Framework or a "Toolbox", so this would be the first chapter where we'll take a look at some of the elements that would be at your disposal, with my recommendations around the order in which to start using them.

Chapter 5 steps into more advanced methods and tools that you could start introducing as an Agile Coach, once you see better acceptance and adoption of core Agile values and practices that you would have introduced to that point.

As evident as it should be, Coaching Journey and organizational change during Transformation will not remain static, requiring you to constantly inspect and adapt to the changing landscape around you.

Chapter 6 talks about Agile Adoption Maturity phase and what it means for both you as a Coach and the organization that is looking for that further step in its transformation.

This is where you as Agile Coach would be more involved with the higher levels of organizational Leadership, formal definition and kick-off of Value Streams, adoption of a Scaling Framework - if your organization and change-championing Team decides that it's a good idea to use one.

Chapter 7 mentions most commonly used and straightforward Agile Adoption Metrics that would help you measure success, and ensure transparency for all affected layers of your organization.

If we don't measure, we don't improve. This slightly simplified view upon the matter of organizational transformations applies very well to your efforts as an Agile Coach assisting the company on its journey towards new ways of working and Continuous Improvement.

In this chapter I will offer you a rather simple model that would be your starting point in helping Teams embrace self-assessment as a practice, as well as spark further discussion and introspection once you could overlay your own Coach's assessment on top of the Teams'.

Chapter 8 helps build understanding of what is a Coaching Definition of Done, as your baseline efforts as Coach would be coming to an end, and it would be time to shift into a slightly different mode of operation.

As opposed to the majority of core Agile Delivery roles, such as Scrum Master, your full-time involvement as an Agile Coach could come to a successful end at one point. In this chapter we will discuss why and when this point will likely come into view and would be worth your consideration as an individual Coach, and as a Community of Practice.

Chapter 9 will serve as a wrap-up for everything we would have discussed in the preceding chapters, and suggest further steps for your professional progress as an Agile Coach.

Here we will discuss my final recommendations, where to from here, suggest further reading and other resources that should help you on your journey to develop into a fully-fledged and all-rounded Agile Coach.

Who is this book for?

While being an Agile Coach myself I'd like to believe that general concepts covered in this book would benefit almost anyone who has something to do with large-scale organizational transformations from traditional methods of delivery to Lean/Agile, there is still certainly a prominent professional angle to all of this - benefiting professionals in some roles a lot more than others.

I'm talking about people currently acting in variety of Digital Project Delivery roles, and who want to either become an Agile Coach, better understand how to work with one, or how to pick the right candidate from the mass of applicants interesting in the job opening that you perhaps advertised.

This summary could translate to any of the following:

- Project and Program Managers
- Digital Delivery Managers
- Scrum Masters or Iteration Managers
- Business Analysts
- Product Managers and Owners
- Corporate Change Managers
- Agile Transformation Leadership
- Heads of Departments affected by Agile Transformation
- Business Owners or Project Sponsors
- Professional Recruiters.

Needless to say that the list above is not exhaustive, but it should give you a good idea if this book would help you in any way.

To put it even simpler:

If you want to better understand how an Agile Coach would help transform your organizational culture towards Agile delivery, starting with basics and progressing towards maturity in broad adoption of Lean Agile practices and methods - this book will benefit you.

If you expect to be working alongside with an Agile Coach or a newly formed

Agile Community of Practice, and want to have an insider view on the typical agenda of such entities in order to help them succeed and reduce the amount of uncertainty stress on your own unit - this book should benefit you as well.

Finally, and most obviously, this book would be of direct benefit to anyone who considers to take their next career step towards the area of Agile Coaching, with little to no idea of where to start, or how coaching practice and methods would be different from a traditional Delivery Manager, or a Scrum Master.

Pre-requisites

To reiterate the obvious one last time - this book is not a Scrum Guide, or some other write-up that teaches you Lean/Agile Fundamentals. As an aspiring Agile Coach you should be very familiar with those, including such bread-and-butter things for people in our industry as Scrum Framework, and essentials of Kanban.

As a Business stakeholder or a professional Recruiter, not directly involved in the matters of Agile Delivery of Project Management, you might benefit from reading the freely available Scrum Guide, and catching up on other materials that would give you a generic idea about Agile versus traditional Waterfall delivery of customer Value.

This book doesn't stop and explain those basics - it assumes you know them, whoever you are. It does however take the reader a few steps further, away from the most well-known processes, frameworks, events and role descriptions that you'd be dealing with already.

You will digest the information given in this book easier if you:

- Have good understanding of Agile Fundamentals, including Scrum framework;

- Have good understanding of what roles exist within typical setup of Agile Project Delivery, and their responsibilities - Developers, Scrum Masters, Product Owners, Product Managers, Business Analysts, User Experience champions and such;

- Have at least basic understanding of Agile Scaling concepts within abstract Digital Delivery setup, such as core terminology and layout of Scaled Agile Framework (SAFe) or Large Scale Scrum (LeSS).

All of the pre-requisite information summarized in bullet points above is freely available on the Internet and should not take you longer than one Google search to find.

2 INTRODUCTION

Becoming a full time Agile Coach is a conscious choice, and an individual journey that might not be for everyone.

So what would prompt you to change your current career and consider becoming an Agile Coach? I hope it's clear without reading this book that in order to become a Coach in any field, you first need to be reasonably good and experienced in the area that you'd like to be coaching in.

Provided you'd want to be taken seriously by professional recruiters on the job market, trying to claim that you are ready for an Agile Coaching role straight out of University, with a freshly printed certificate of a Professional Scrum Master is out of question - you could save yourself the time and embarrassment.

Likely scenario however would be if you are already a Scrum Master, Product Owner, Delivery Manager, or an Agile Project Manager of some kind, who feels like they are ready for next step and are unsatisfied for some reason with what you are currently doing. Because desire to overcome your current role limitations and do more, changing your field of work perhaps, or "stepping up" in some way are some of the key drivers of change that majority of us would have to deal with in our professional lives.

As Agile professional space grew exponentially over the last 10 or so years, qualifying someone as a valid Agile Coach who is able to help your organization became even harder than before - whether you are considering to hire one, or trying to professionally pivot yourself on the market as a job candidate.

Current state of Agile Coaching job market around Australia at the end of 2017 and beginning of 2018 is resembling the American Wild West a little, where with increasing regularity you see yet another black hat character riding into town with an intent that's yet to be seen by the townsfolk...

I'm making the picture a bit more dramatic deliberately, but it is accurate regardless, if you do some research, and look at the facts.

Digital Delivery established itself rather solidly across Australian corporate landscape, some baseline practices have been around for a few years too, where all "Agile" efforts are being spearheaded by already quite plentiful workforce of Scrum Masters.

As Scrum is quite easy to understand and follow with some due diligence, there is also no shortage of professionals quite competent in the other Scrum-friendly roles, such as Product Owners.

Proper practice of Agile Coaching is another cup of tea altogether.

Mainly because there is no such thing as a well-known, documented, and accepted Agile Coaching Framework, that one could just download (preferably free!) from the Internet, follow to the letter like Scrum Guide - and call themselves an Agile Coach on the other end of this experience.

I'm stressing the "well-known" point in the paragraph above, because there are certainly emerging bodies that try and establish themselves as central governing bodies of knowledge surrounding proper Agile Coaches training and accreditation.

This book is not specifically designed about thoroughly analyzing your options of getting employed as a Coach and becoming efficient from virtually day-one, hitting the ground running once you've been through rigorous training and certifications that some of those organizations claim to provide.

Instead, it focuses on my own practical experience of building up my knowledge and becoming an Agile Coach, exchanging findings and recommendations with similar trailblazers in the field - not in a shiny classroom (not to say there's anything wrong with classrooms).

Having Scrum to thank and blame at the same time for popularity and misunderstanding surrounding concepts of Agile out there, I'll have to refer to Scrum very frequently when comparing whole range of relevant things such as methods of influencing stakeholders, training the teams, and how much creativity the role of a classic Scrum Master requires versus someone who claims to be an Agile Coach.

Throughout the book I'll be using my own recommendation to not be afraid to repeat yourself as you are trying to instill positive change in your organization as a Coach, tackling the same concept or approach from different angles and trying to make sure it settles well in your mind as a reader.

As I mentioned earlier, process of becoming an Agile Coach is a choice followed by a substantial self-education effort that starts with a solid base level of core Agile knowledge (modern landscape, prominent frameworks, values, principles, effective practices given certain circumstances, etc.), assisted by hopefully decent understanding of how an adult education and learning processes work.

You will have to accept that constant pursuit of further knowledge and feedback on your own efforts and performance will have to become your second nature, and that it might take months and years before you will feel comfortable to remove that slash from your job title with "Agile Coach" label appended, and simply call yourself an Agile Coach, with no hints of being a professional hybrid.

This Introduction is not intended to scare you off, or to create some vision of an unreachable mountain peak ahead of you - far from it.

But I've always been a straight-shooter and an honest speaker, so creating realistic expectations about what kind of journey you are looking at if you'd like to give becoming an Agile Coach a proper shot is of paramount importance to me.

The goal of this book is to arm you with as much information relevant to someone just starting their Agile Coaching career as possible, giving you the right tools to do the job while no other solid guidance is available, and then letting you figure out the rest and pursue further knowledge - as there's plenty of it to be gained.

How I became an Agile Coach

To give you further context of who I am and how my own Agile Coaching career started, I've decided to include this section of my background story, as it might not be that different to yours...

I've made my early career path decisions following what I thought were simple and logical principles - looking at what I was professionally interested in at that time, choosing the closest job title from what was available on the market, and then pursuing the advertised option until I received my next job offer.

I've never remained static for too long however, learning rapidly and regularly challenging myself in whether or not my current duties continued satisfying me professionally, staying aligned with the further career milestones I've penciled in for myself.

Starting my career from the most accessible point that aligned with my interests at that time which was Software Development, I rather quickly figured out that developing the invisible nuts and bolts of the complex software systems was not my thing at all.

I was more interested in the visual part of the products we were building at that time, implicitly interacting with the End-User, better understanding their needs and challenges, and making their digital life easier. That led me into Web User Interface development, where I spent a few early years of my professional life.

Personality and possibly a bit of luck helped me get into team leadership roles, where I was feeling most satisfaction from making sure everyone was okay with what they were doing, all technical requirements were well understood, workload sharing was sorted out sensibly - with no particular method at that time, just using common sense and input from Team members.

That was around the time when Agile first appeared on my radar as a new buzz-word.

First wave of industry-wide Agile teachings was already spreading of course, it just took a while back then to penetrate thick walls of timeline-driven software development, especially in very rigid legacy environments such as Swiss banks and Insurance companies I used to work for.

Once I discovered that the "new ways of working" movement existed, I dived into whatever learnings were available at the time. I've attended developer conferences and started reading blogs of people who started properly practicing Agile methods such as Scrum.

That was the phase when I was absorbing as much information from the experts of that time, who certainly knew more than I did about the matter at hand, ran brown bag sessions and various trainings trying to share their knowledge with the rest of us - new Agile enthusiasts.

Some more time passed and I found myself at a fork road in the road, where it became clear that working with people and optimizing the way Teams work meant more to me than writing cleaner and more efficient code.

That led to the first major pivot in my career, where I plotted my way towards Agile Delivery and eventually becoming a Scrum Master via more easily accessible role of a Technical Agile Business Analyst.

Looking back at that time I see that period as the infancy of my own understanding of how Agile project teams should be structured and work within realistic corporate conditions, outside of a clean classroom where they teach you about Scrum, even virtually - online.

Cutting to the chase here a little bit, the problem of most classic Agile organizational guides including Scrum is that quite often those are detached from reality and challenges of our organizations, that are most likely going to benefit from those methods being implemented correctly.

That understanding did not come to me straight away, but over a couple more years of practicing Agile methods (mostly Scrum, with occasional attempts to scale up) and attempting to assist the teams enabling efficient and predictable delivery while maintaining quality of the product, and seeing most of those attempts spectacularly fail most of the time.

Now I firmly believe that unless you've been in the trenches of digital delivery attempting to utilize picture-perfect Scrum guidelines to the letter, without major tectonic cultural shifts in the setup of the organization itself including its leadership, and seeing those fail for a whole range of easy to articulate reasons, you'd be unfit to convincingly teach others, or expect them to succeed at what they are doing.

That was the lightbulb moment for me where I finally realized what I would like to do for the foreseeable future of my career. I saw large number of people seriously struggling with the freshly announced corporate enterprise-scale transformations trying to figure out what did that mean to them - with all the announced changes to their roles, responsibilities and expectations of their management.

Luckily large-scale organizations trying to embrace Agile saw a need to create an additional layer of roles that were close to Delivery Teams but weren't classified as Management per se. Those were known as Iteration Manager and Delivery Manager. I've been in both of those roles in more than one organization.

I was not wrong thinking that my newly chosen career path would give me a sense of satisfaction, helping people in the affected delivery teams with adoption of agile methods. However as the time went on and as my knowledge of most commonly used Agile delivery methods increased, most custom (*usually meaning - incomplete, due to organizational and other constraints out of my control at that time*) implementations of Scrum and other methods such as Lean Kanban started appearing to me more obviously lopsided and sub-optimal.

I caught myself thinking more and more often that me doing my job as that custom implementation of an Agile Delivery Manager role actually deviated and even detracted from the goals that I thought my organization should have been aiming for.

After all, the need for those roles within transforming organizations meant that there was a certain structural or functional gap that my role was designed to *cover up*, rather than make sure that the new structure didn't have that gap and the need for such custom "adapter" role in the first place.

I was conflicted because at that point I fully realized that picture-perfect textbook implementations of recommended Agile practices didn't always work even if someone insisted on obeying the rules the rules to the letter. At the same time continuing to help the organization survive doing the "wrong thing", supporting the broken and outdated status-quo by continuing to perform my custom (and not really Agile) role was also hardly the best way forward for me.

In addition to those realizations I felt that I already had enough practical and theoretical knowledge that filled me with confidence to be ready for another chapter in my career, now focusing on optimizing the Lean Agile practices of the organization as opposed to continuing to deal with the matters and issues surrounding timely project delivery.

That is how I decided to bite the bullet and call myself an Agile Coach one sunny day. Running ahead of myself here a little bit, I'll go ahead and tell you that I don't think there's one very specific point at which you'll feel like you are "100% ready" for the new title.

I've observed enough people acting in Agile Coaching roles at various times, where I quietly disagreed with their methods in many ways and observed what I saw as fundamental disregard to what the cultural reality of the organization demanded at that time.

Those "pseudo-coaches" were rigid in their understanding of what was right for the company and the people, charging ahead like bulls following direct orders from the clueless leadership, not having the guts to coach the people running the show, as well as the Teams.

They were part of the problem I thought we were all there to solve, spinning the wheels and turning into disregarded shadow roles that not many people respected.

I didn't think I knew better than them on all accounts of sheer knowledge of numerous Agile methods and practices, but truly believed that I could come up with alternatives to offer the tired crowd of people who were rapidly losing faith in the process, becoming more and more negatively vocal about what they thought was "Agile", and how they felt about organizational transformations in general.

Fast forwarding my story to present time, in this book I would like to offer you my take on the life of an Agile Coach joining a transforming organization, from the perspective of making the most Positive Impact in the least amount of time, while causing the least amount of stress to themselves and the people they'd be working with.

Some extra scene-setting

In the following chapters, we will start by talking about the obvious things first - such as the differences between most common Agile project delivery roles and that of an Agile Coach.

Having done this role transition myself I know for a fact that's some concepts, focus points, and other elements of Agile Coaching role are simply too obscure for you to notice just yet - if for instance you are transitioning into the role from being a Scrum Master, Project Manager, or anyone else coming from a solid Delivery background.

I believe that as someone who has done this transition myself I'd be able to articulate some important points to you as early as possible, to make sure you don't struggle as much during arguably the most difficult part of your career pivot - as you just start your new coaching role.

Once the setting of the scene is out of the way, I will tell you about is the typical Agile Coaching journey as far as your organization is concerned, which should create a foundation for your self-driven educated assessment of what tools and methods would be applicable in your coaching efforts going forward.

Finally we will spend quite some time going through the actual basic Agile Coaching Framework that I sometimes referred to as "Toolbox", because coaching methods we use are varied and plentiful. Seeing them as part of that virtual toolbox that is at your disposal seems to be one of the easiest methods to nudge you in the direction of the right mindset, without limiting you too much in your own journey of professional self-discovery.

After all we discover what works for us and what doesn't which is especially true when we talk about such advanced interpersonal stuff as unobtrusive day-to-day coaching of adult professionals.

I believe reading this book would be of benefit to not just aspiring Agile Coaches but also a broad range of professionals who find themselves being part of an unfolding Agile transformation of their company.

It might be just as important for a business executive or someone in another company leadership role feeling the need to bring an educated Agile influencer on board to better understand what a professional Agile Coach could do for them, how could they help, how do they need to be supported in order to start that positive cultural shift.

Because if I could teach you one thing right now it would be that an Agile Coach cannot do it all alone. Being supported by the company leadership and change management are paramount success factors for an Agile Coach starting to work at your company.

Then there is the purpose of educating various hiring professionals in what to look for when trying to fill a role of an Agile Coach for your organization, or on behalf of one, as an external Recruiter.

How to tell a good one from an imposter candidate?

In broad and advanced areas such as Agile Coaching it is virtually impossible to tell if you are short-listing the right candidate for the job based purely on the look of their Resume. Also, gone are the days when your basic questions about components of Scrum framework would substantially help you filter out the good from the bad, as that knowledge became too mainstream…

So among other things in this book, I will try and help you form a better picture what's the right professional attitude and skill-set that should be demonstrated by an Agile Coaching role applicant, to give you reasonable confidence in that they know what they are talking about and that they won't waste your Teams' and Leadership's time, until they find their feet and even better align with strategic goals of your organization.

3 AGILE COACH VS SCRUM MASTER

Let us continue by discussing the key differences between the role of an Agile Coach and a Trainer. While these two labels are often used interchangeably, I believe there is subtle but fundamental differences understanding which will help you succeed in the role of an Agile Coach.

Agile (or most commonly Scrum) Trainer is someone who focuses more on the theory of how to do things right. It is someone who we could easily imagine running training sessions in a classroom of sorts, then leaving the trainees to go and implement the learnings as they see fit.

Coach however would be someone looking after the team of people over a prolonged period of time, teaching them how to do things better, helping them learn, and pushing them in the right direction when required. Coach could also run training sessions but the role is much broader than that of a Trainer. So in essence Trainer is the more theory-focused short interaction role, while the coach is more hands-on, practical and constantly present person.

Both Trainer and Coach have knowledge to give to the group of people, but Trainer works in a "sprint mode" and Coach sees their efforts as a marathon. Agile Coach aims to establish the learning process among people they are working with, understanding that *it will take time* for the new working culture to settle like second nature among the affected Teams.

Trainer however knows that they don't have much time to convey whatever knowledge it is they are offering to the attendees of their training session. So they prepare and package that knowledge in the most digestible bite-sized chunks they believe would be easy to grasp in the short-term, making the most impact if implemented and practiced soon after the training is complete.

Good Trainers appreciate the value of a well-established learning process among their "students", but remain well aware that they don't have the luxury of time to make sure that learning process is in place, and neither they'd be present daily to help guide that learning process further, helping the team every step of the way. Coach on the other hand has that luxury of time, provided they are set up for success by their organization.

So as you can see, the differences are actually substantial if you look at both roles a bit closer.

Now let's talk about the differences between Agile Coach and Scrum Master. These should be much easier to spot I believe.

Scrum Master's intended purpose is in the name of the role. Masters of Scrum are embedded in the Teams, specializing in Scrum Framework and also acting as a "light version" of an Agile Coach. Except their focus is limited to Scrum practices and ensuring the team is set up and supported the best way possible for them to meet their commitments.

Scrum Master is a delivery role. While it has substantial element of education in its responsibilities, particulars of Scrum are not the hardest subject to teach, especially if you are present in the Team space every day. Scrum Masters are also the first point of escalation of any issues that the Team cannot resolve itself.

To summarize, Scrum Master is an educator and pacemaker specializing in Scrum. In larger transforming organizations Scrum Masters are often asked to do more than their classically prescribed duties. It especially happens when company's Transformation Office (there's often one) is still new to Agile methods, and is relying on custom "hybrid" roles and responsibilities dictated by the persistent needs and limitations of their slowly transforming organization. In the interest of staying on topic, we will not dive deep into those additional hybrid responsibilities of a Scrum Master role right now.

Compared to a Scrum Master, an Agile Coach is someone who knows more than just Scrum, and spends a lot of time talking to individuals and groups in a certain way that induces the right state of mind, embracing Agile values and Continuous Improvement culture.

It is someone who shifted their focus from the matters of Delivery to looking at organizational transformation as a whole process. Agile Coach typically is proficient with more than just one delivery method, being experienced enough to assess organizational situation and educate the teams on what method would suit their needs best at any given point in time.

In addition to the key differences between Agile Delivery and Training roles from Agile Coaching that we've discussed above, the goals of a Coach and the way we try and induce a positive cultural change in people we work with are different.

At a very high level, generic Agile Coaching approach and goals could be summarized by the following three points:

1. Show them how to do it
2. See them repeat and do it themselves
3. See them grow enough to start teaching others

It is up to the coach to determine what method or tool that would be best suited given the current Agile adoption level within the organization, and then kick-off the practice of using that tool or method leading by example.

Setting the right vector for the teams you are coaching, and then letting them repeat, practice and make mistakes - are foundational pieces of basic learning process that you as a coach are there to ignite.

Being with the teams, and coaching individuals throughout the organizational transformation where required, would hopefully lead you to the point where you'll see the people you've coached become so comfortable with the subject matter, that they'd display behaviors of their own voluntary learning within related Lean Agile disciplines and knowledge areas.

This is where you are likely to see emerging champions who effectively picked up where you left off, carrying the flag forward and attempting to proactively teach others, while improving the depth of their own knowledge.

As an Agile Coach just starting out, or a Leader employing a new Coach, you would also benefit from considering the following points as early as possible:

1. Your coaching efforts usually yield better results with permanent staff, who are more invested in the cultural change and their position within the company;

2. While adoption of basic practices might happen quickly, there will be an almost inevitable "plateau of visible progress", that might look very discouraging to you and the leaders of your organization, who might be getting impatient for big bang results;

3. As a Coach you will be in business of repeating yourself, over and over. As a role more focused on establishment of the new organizational culture, you will have to employ full range of learning process techniques, starting with the good-old classic - "Repetition is a mother of learning".

4. To further reinforce point #2 above, expect the cultural Change to happen slowly. On-boarding a Coach, or becoming one within an

organization is a long-term investment from both sides - of an individual performing the role, and the company that welcomes a Coach to join their ranks.

This is not to say that knowing the few points singled out above would now give you full range of the view you need to consider yourself a fully established Agile Coach.

This book dives into more topics as the narrative continues, but I trust this should serve as a solid departure point for your journey on improving your knowledge and understanding further.

4 SETTING UP FOR SUCCESS

End-to-end success of the organizational transformation is not solely in Agile Coach's hands. As obvious as this statement reads, there is no way to overstate the importance of organizational readiness to give the new ways of working that Coach brings with them a proper try.

In other words, an on-boarded Agile Coach needs to be set up for success by the Leadership and both sides of a typical organization - Business and Information Technology (IT) - in order to succeed in their efforts of changing the culture in a positive and sustainable way.

Additionally, and at any organizational scale, companies and programs of work employing a new Coach need to better understand what the Coach could do for them, and what kind of internal set-up and support would be required for that Coach to be most efficient.

All of the above could be summarized as simply as not everything is in Coach's hands.

Research and working practice show that there are a few most prominent factors that usually impact an Agile Coach, both positively and negatively. In this chapter I'll talk you through those, giving as much relevant context for each as I can.

Factor 1- Buy-in

Buy-in from Business Leadership of your organization. Not much will happen without it.

Business is supposed to be the Customer facing side of Agile Delivery Set-up, they will provide guidance on Product priorities, clarity of purpose and requirements, and acceptance of the work as "Done".

Their desire to learn and improve in their methods of interaction with (usually) Information Technology units delivering on their requirements needs to be there from get-go. They need to be motivated, preferably not just extrinsically, in order for you to succeed as a Coach and people investing into Lean Agile culture of your organization.

Business needs to be brought into this usually IT-driven initiative as early as possible, trained and coached along the way, breaking the old habit of throwing requirements over the wall and forgetting about those until the Project delivery date.

Factor 2- Time

Change happens slowly. As I've mentioned in the previous sections, a Coach needs time to establish the right culture and help grow it.

In the optimal scenario of organizational buy-in into Agile transformation, you can expect around 6 months before Agile Fundamentals and base-level Agile practices will be properly adopted, with Teams being relatively self-sufficient in those rituals, practices, starting to embrace Agile way of thinking.

Management might not expect this - best way to avoid disappointment down the track is to be clear and upfront about what is going to happen, and how long - on average - it will take.

Factor 3 - Project Funding

While it might not be your job or area of expertise as a Coach to provide specific recommendations on establishment of the new funding model, raising this question early with your Leadership is important.

Project-based funding on scope that is not negotiable and set in stone, and immovable delivery dates for the whole 100% complete end result would kill your Agile transformation efforts without a chance of recovery.

Your job as a Coach would be to explain to your Leadership the difference between Product view upon delivery of customer Value, and the traditional Project Management approach. Encouraging creation of a funding model where scope is seen as the negotiable part in a healthy and reliable process of Digital Delivery, enabling inspection and adaptation at both Program and Team levels would be a big win on your journey towards the new ways of working.

Left unchanged in the long run, traditional Project approval and funding models could become the single reason why your Teams weren't able to adopt the Agile values or methods of delivery.

After all, you'll be teaching them to estimate the incoming work, and commit only to the amounts they think they could deliver according to priorities set by their Product Owner, while the Project Management Office (which is usually the last element of traditionally operated organization to die) would keep insisting on delivery of fully signed-off scope by the dates that were committed without any input from delivery Teams at the start of the Project.

You can't have a good Soccer game if the judges are scoring you according to the rules of Basketball… I hope this makes sense!

Factor 4- Needing Help

You can't do this alone. Agile Coach could "start the fire", run the initial training, and kick-off cadence of coaching sessions with the impacted Delivery Teams and stakeholders, but it's highly unlikely that they'd be able to see the whole Agile transformation through as a solo effort.

There's just too much to do, across the organizational layers and delivery teams, if you are genuinely trying to do this right, without omitting something significant and cutting too many corners.

Even before recruiting more professional Agile Coaches, starting to identify local Agile champions within the Teams is usually a very good start to building a strong and self-sustaining Agile Practice and culture.

Factor 5- Communities of Practice

Section above leads to the expansion into creation of a Community of Practice.

Identifying motivated "helpers", professionals who are capable and willing to learn and improve their knowledge of Agile, step up and develop themselves - will pay off tenfold in most Agile transformation scenarios.

Factor 6- Needing Training

Coaches also need training and further self-development. As a coach, invest time and resources into upskilling in the professional areas that you feel like you need a boost in.

As an employer, offer the coach some opportunities, time, and ideally budget to attend courses, conferences, meetups that help build their Community of Practice and professional capability that would benefit your organization.

Factor 7- Seeking Feedback

Finally, as a Coach, seek feedback. Don't remain in the isolation of the personal perception bubble. External input, however less educated than your own, could be of benefit to you - informing you on how your efforts are perceived from outside, as well as potential helpful pointers you were genuinely not aware of.

This is certainly not an exhaustive list of all factors that might impact success chances of you as an Agile Coach, or of your Coach from the perspective of a Leader who felt that they need one.

But it should serve as a good start, while you are still trying to build a big picture around your new role.

5 COACHING JOURNEY OUTLINE

Let's expand on the three main points of a classic Coaching Approach that I've given you in the previous chapters, and create a typical outline for a Coaching Journey within your organization, to help guide your vision further.

To reset the stage, I'm assuming that we are looking at:

- An Agile Coach who is new to the role, with no better time-proven methods that they'd prefer to rely on, seeking that initial boost of confidence and direction of their coaching efforts;

- An organization that is new to Agile methods and practices.

The typical Agile Coaching journey you are likely looking at will consist of the two virtual phases, that I'll label - "Basics" and "Maturity".

This split isn't a strict 50/50, and the duration of each phase will heavily depend on the size and particulars of your organization that's about to undertake an Agile transformation.

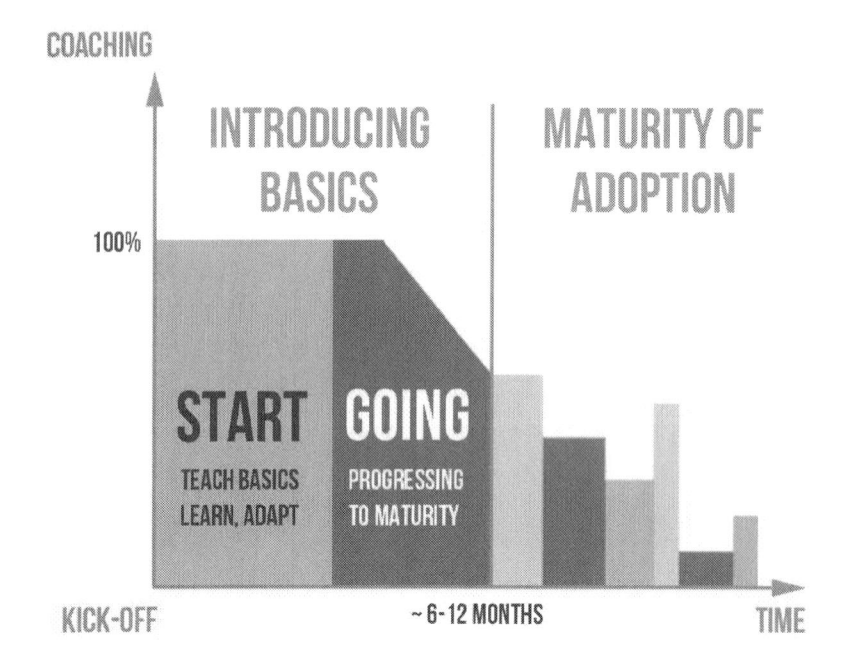

[Figure: Coaching effort over time, showing "Introducing Basics" phase (Start: Teach Basics, Learn, Adapt; Going: Progressing to Maturity) from Kick-off through ~6-12 months at 100%, transitioning to "Maturity of Adoption" phase with decreasing coaching levels over time.]

We will discuss each phase in detail, and further chapters of this book will add to the picture above.

Basics Adoption Phase

As the title suggests, this is the initial phase that starts with Agile transformation kick-off activities as those are seen by your organization or a Program of work (as smaller-scale undertaking), where you'll be preoccupied by laying the foundation for Agile culture, with some basic practices and activities.

I've separated Basics phase into two sub-phases, which once again do not have to form an even split at the end of the day.

"Start" Sub-Phase

This is where you are likely to be looking at a real greenfield environment, with your Teams and Leadership not knowing much about Agile, where you only start training them up in Fundamentals and teaching them real basics.

Your goal as Agile Coach should be to get introduced to the Teams and key stakeholders that these teams interact with, better understand the ways they currently work, form your own understanding of what their "base level" of Agile knowledge is.

This is also where you aim to conduct or attend Agile Fundamentals training with your teams. You need to build trust and kick-off a relationship with multiple layers of your organization or Program of work that will be impacted by your upcoming activities as you start nudging everyone in the right direction of new ways of working.

As far as key methods are concerned, your weapon of choice during this initial phase is likely to be Scrum - unsurprisingly - due to how clearly laid out the framework is, with prescribed roles, responsibilities and rituals that were designed to put the Teams and interacting stakeholders into the right frame of mind.

As a Coach you could assess the nature of work the Teams are doing and recommend going for Lean Kanban straight away, but arguably it would be much harder for you to establish the right cadence and rules of the game then, due to how much more loosely Kanban practice is regulated (e.g. there are even no specifically prescribed Roles in Kanban).

"Going" or "Progressing" Sub-Phase

This would be the time when you as a coach start observing the Leadership using the right language when communicating with Business and Technical stakeholders, interacting more with the Delivery Teams.

At the same time the Teams themselves should start displaying some autonomy in running basic events such as full range of Scrum Framework rituals, as they demonstrate visible progress towards Agile Adoption Maturity.

Your involvement as a coach here could start shifting upward, towards forming more solid layer of Agile-aware Program Management, provided this wasn't in place when you've just started your journey and had to concentrate your single-coach limited efforts on laying the foundation at the Team level.

During the whole "Basics Adoption" phase I'd expect your almost 100% allocation to the Delivery Teams you'd have to look after, in order to observe them as closely as you could, letting them get used to you more, as you start transforming the space around you towards increased Agility of operation.

While we'll review recommended activities and specific stress-points that would be worth your while as a Coach during this transformational phase, in this summary I'll recommend your attendance of all framework-recommended rituals (such as Daily Scrum and Sprint Planning).

You might need to be acting Scrum Master for a little while, even if they have one currently in place, to help them get into the right working mode and show the best practice of running those events, before letting them explore and make mistakes on their own.

Coming from Delivery side of Digital Project Management, it is especially important to slow down and fully embrace the new viewpoint where you are a teacher, and a person who is there to establish a continuous learning and improvement culture. While you'll be constantly tempted to keep giving your Teams the right answer and boost their progress along the way, this is not necessarily the best way to help them learn.

Showing them the way, and letting them continue on the journey making their own mistakes as they learn the ropes, while smartly pointing out where they could have done better - would serve as a much more solid foundation for your Agile Coaching practice and habits you should be working to develop.

Your immediate allocation to the Teams might start winding down a little bit, as by the time Maturity of Agile Adoption phase starts you'd expect to have Scrum Masters trained and capable enough to handle most of day-to-day stuff you had to deal with when just starting off.

Maturity of Agile Adoption

As I compiled my initial research findings and prepared the phase breakdown diagram above, I was leaning towards a more optimistic assessment that under good circumstances Maturity of Agile adoption phase might begin as early as 6 months from the Transformation kick-off.

Looking at more facts, my own experience, and talking to many of my colleagues from different industries, I'm more inclined to bump that virtual phase-shift line to **12 months** mark.

This is when you as a Coach should start seeing a consistent display of behaviors and delivery-related activity, suggesting that Agile Fundamentals and basics of Continuous Improvement culture are in place, without any need for your constant supervision or intervention.

So what specifically should you expect to be in place by the time this "Agile Adoption Maturity" phase begins?

Basics Are In Place

This could include (but doesn't have to be limited to) the following:

1. Agile Fundamentals Training completed for all Teams and

Leadership affected by Agile Transformation initiative;

2. Delivery Teams that will be adopting new ways of working identified, assembled, with all mandatory roles filled and responsibilities of those well understood;

3. In case of Scrum being selected as core delivery Framework, cadence of Sprints planned and communicated across the whole Program of work, with all prescribed events and rituals being in place;

4. Business stakeholders, including Sponsor and Program Management keenly accepting new ways of working, attending Sprint Reviews and eager to provide feedback on what Teams are demonstrating as increments of produced Value;

5. Communities of Practice are being formed for key knowledge groups such as Product Owners (and/or Agile Business Analysts), Scrum Masters (and/or generally Agile Practitioners of the Organization);

6. Cross-functionality of Delivery Teams is improving with easily observable dynamics such as knowledge-sharing sessions organized by Developers, brown-bag sessions, catch-ups, and similar learning events showing that new Agile-friendly culture has sunken into the organization.

Leadership is open about their Vision

Arguably one of the points that belong in pre-requisites of any Agile Transformation that wants to be a success, I'm emphasizing this once again as a milestone that is required before you could consider organization properly "Mature" in their adoption of Agile and new ways of working, being prepared for further knowledge boost and operational up-scaling.

Leadership of the organization should be open about communicating their Program Vision with all affected layers, and preferably doing it not via Change Management's Emails once every couple of weeks, but some sort of face-to-face sessions with the Teams, their actual visibility on the ground, perhaps attending Team's Sprint Review from time to time as guests.

By this phase you as Agile Coach should have established some contact with direct Leadership responsible for this Agile Transformation, knowing first-hand about how they see this Vision evolving in the closest future.

Likely More Than One Coach

Given our earlier assumption that we are talking about medium-to-large scale Agile Transformation that you are assisting with as a new Agile Coach, and still presuming that typical direction of scaling up operations on the ground is part of Leadership's vision for the organization, you would want to see more than just yourself pushing this cart up the proverbial hill.

If we keep going with this hypothetical and fairly common scenario, you are unlikely to succeed with "Maturity" phase alone, even though your direct involvement in simple day-to-day Agile rituals such as Scrum events might reduce significantly.

This is the phase where you'll have to start taking proactive steps in introducing Agile Scaling concepts, perhaps helping your organization pick a Framework that will describe methods of scaling more formally, introducing new set of rules and layers of roles.

It's worth pausing here and addressing any concerns that you might have with my implicit recommendation and default direction towards introduction of a Scaling Framework, as soon as your organization appears to be out of the woods of Agile Basics adoption.

There are multiple and evolving views upon the subject of whether or not a generic organization actually needs a formal Agile Scaling Framework in place, and there are plenty of good reasons for this debate.

More and more Agile champions vote for bulky Agile Scaling Frameworks being another buzz-word and inflated requirement of Transformations, while according to them simple basic common sense-driven coordination of efforts and dependencies between individual Scrum Teams would satisfy 90% of the companies who are currently bothering with scaling complexities that they don't really need.

I'm in agreement with both sides of this virtual debate, simply trying to emphasize the main rule you should always have in mind as an Agile Coach or even a Change Manager of your organization: pick the right tools for the right job, and get the basics established first.

I've consulted for companies that insisted on a roll-out of some Scaling Framework from the first moment of kicking off their Agile Transformation. There was brief assessment done, based purely on numbers of people within the organization and complexity of managerial layers that "needed a job in the new world", which was a reason enough to those companies to make up their minds there and then, not really looking at things closely enough.

I'm against that approach, and believe it is the main reason why majority of such rushed "tickbox transformations" fail. They feel they have to do it "because company A did it, and we are not worse than them!" I won't even start explaining here why this shows a real legacy 1950s prescriptive Project and Program Management approach, and why it shouldn't have a place in the new world that we live in.

The opposite end of the spectrum of course are those companies that are reluctant to look beyond the real basic level of Agile adoption, such as roll-out of Scrum framework at the lowest level of individual Delivery Teams, and making no effort to try and assist with some Program level coordination, setting a cohesive vision, or planning the work while "zooming out" for a better vantage point.

Both extremes are bad.

As I've mentioned in the Introduction chapter of this book, telling you a bit more about my own background story, I'm a big fan and proponent of common sense based on education and experience, when it comes to planning next strategic steps for your transforming organization.

There are tools and methods that you could utilize if specific conditions within your organization are right for those, and the specialists you invest into should be there to help assess those needs.

One of the key roles in this assessment is naturally that of an Agile Coach - the one you are either aspiring to be, or the one you've just decided to hire. Regardless of the exact case, the point I'm making here is that you could almost never go wrong if you focus on getting basics straight, letting the new culture settle in, and then seeing how exactly you'd like to scale this up - if it's at all required for your company.

6 COACHING FRAMEWORK – START

Finally we are at the point where enough theory was given to you in order to start thinking like an Agile Coach, planning out their work for the foreseeable transformation journey of your organization.

Now we could start going through specific Coaching Services, or the "Tools of the Trade" that you should have at your disposal for various phases of Agile Adoption Maturity and Phase of organizational transformation.

We will start with the things you should do or pay attention to as Agile Coach during the very start of your coaching journey, and the Introducing Basics phase. As a ground rule for the most effective tools of this phase, you will mostly use those **pro**actively, rather than **re**actively.

This meaningful division of what you'll end up having in your personal coaching toolbox will help you take the right approach when having little time for deep analysis of what might be required. Some of the methods, rituals and ways to go about things as a Coach would scream proactive use at you, while others will leave no doubt that it's an "upon request" type of activity.

After this quick scene-setting, let's dive straight into the core tools for your starting out phase.

Agile Fundamentals Training

Point number one, almost without exception, unless you are joining the company as a new Agile Coach after this initial kick-off phase has passed.

Lucky you in that case - as there would be less for you to do, including breaking the initial resistance barrier that's inevitable from a large portion of individuals undergoing such organizational transformation - however the downside here would be that you'd miss out on being with the teams front and center, when they arguably needed you the most as a Coach.

Continuing with our hypothetical situation, let's assume it is a complete Greenfield, and you came in as a Coach needing to start everything from zero. I personally prefer this kind of setup, even with all the challenges of having zero positive momentum, as this allows you to bond with your Teams and Leadership much better than someone jumping in at a later stage.

The choice of how to conduct Fundamentals training will end up being up to you as Agile Coach on the ground, and the Leadership that is responsible for overall delivery of this Transformation.

If it's a relatively small scale, it might be worth doing this yourself, or pairing up with a fellow Agile Coach from your organization - if you have another one. This also assumes you've had some prior experience training up groups of people, which means not just speaking comfortably in front of an audience, but delivering 1-2 days of structured content that you must also have handy as background PowerPoint slides and the rehearsed accompanying narrative.

Reality check-point:

Even without significant experience training up groups of people as described above, you should feel reasonably comfortable in the situation of needing to step into the shoes of an Agile/Scrum Trainer, and conduct an all-day session on Agile Fundamentals. While this is not a day-to-day job of an Agile Coach, it's a prominent element of what we might need to do, and the simplest way to be honest with yourself - gauging whether or not you are ready to call yourself an Agile Coach.

Company-wide Agile Fundamentals training is usually conducted by an external company specializing in those trainings.

It is a larger-scale undertaking in terms of effort, also having some obvious benefits, such as the effect of a completely neutral and experienced body that has no history with your organization, which is often perceived as having more authority in what they'll be teaching your people.

Plus, as you might agree having dealt with professional services in almost any area - one thing is knowing how to DIY fix your kitchen sink, and another one is to be doing it for a living multiple times a day...

I would also recommend that you attended the externally-conducted training of your teams as a Coach, as this would help the teams to feel supported and accompanied by you on their transformation journey from day one, allowing you to become a fellow participant in the exercises, seeing first-hand how the external trainer decided to deliver those basic concepts.

You might be able to fill in some gaps answering questions about how something discussed in abstract sense would fit into your organization. External trainer won't be able to give your teams that perspective, and you should aim to do exactly that, even if it turns out to be just taking notes, and promising the team members to get back to them with the answers later.

Conducting Team Skills Assessment

Continuing to assume a Greenfield situation where you are "on your own" in setting everyone off on their journey the right way, conducting an initial skills-assessment at Team level would be a good idea.
There are multiple ways to run this exercise, but generally it would take you between one and two hours, with some preparation done upfront.

General idea behind any skills assessment is to find out how equipped your teams are to deal with the tasks requiring certain skill-set, as far as delivery of Customer Value is concerned within the new assembly of co-located developers who would have a goal of becoming properly cross-functional Agile teams in near future.

Skills assessment could help you achieve or significantly progress towards a few more prominent goals:

1. Agree with Teams what skills are perceived necessary to succeed in the current phase of Agile transformation, as well as efficiently deliver Customer Value;

2. Identify skill-gaps that require your attention as Agile Coach to ensure further adoption of new methods and practices goes smoothly;

3. Identify local champions and potential mentors who would be keen to assist their fellow Team-mates in developing their own skills further, basically giving you as a Coach free helping hands that would serve as amplifiers of what you'd be trying to achieve across many more Teams.

As basic format of the exercise, you would generally get together with your Leadership Team or already established Agile Community of Practice and come up with the initial list of skills that are most important and relevant at this initial kick-off phase.

Then you'd circulate this list of skills between the Teams - perhaps making it visible on the company's collaboration tool such as Wiki/Confluence, and sending a link around - requesting review and feedback if any of the skills are missing in anyone's view.

I would then create a template that could probably be just a table or a grid, with relevant skills being listed in the first column, one skill per row, and the level of proficiency in that skill would be represented by more columns following the first one.

In one of the following chapters about **Agile Adoption Metrics** I'm giving example of a table-template used to gauge Team's self-assessment of their Agile practices. That exercise serves a different purpose and takes Team view, rather than how each individual Team member assesses their own skill-set. But as far as visual format goes - I'd say it would be close to what you could come up with here.

Once your template is ready, you ask each individual team member to do that self-assessment of their skills before the actual get-together exercise happens.

During the exercise I would normally start by recapping what exactly each skill listed on the template meant to us when we prepared for the exercise. Here you could gauge if there are any discrepancies in understanding, and if any team-members would like to re-vote on their skills, now that any possible confusion was cleared up.

I would explain that current marks that team members gave themselves are reflecting their present day view of themselves. This is where I'd encourage the group to break into pairs, to allow discussion of their own results with their colleagues. If the Team you are conducting this exercise with is relatively large, I wouldn't prevent grouping of more than 2 individual team members for discussion.

Then an important point would be to request everyone to use a differently colored pen, and mark their aspiration level for each relevant skill. For example if you've scored yourself at level "2" on Understanding of Agile

Fundamentals, this could be your chance to put a differently colored "5" for the same skill, indicating that you are interested in learning more and developing yourself in this skill area further.

This is where a little coffee break would serve well, letting people relax and regroup a bit, talking between themselves, while you as a Coach would normally stick individual skill matrices (those printed out table-templates) on a wall.

Putting those next to each other increases visibility and opens up Part 2 of such workshop, where everyone could spend some time looking at others' marks, eventually identifying similarities in skill gaps and learning aspirations.

You could then ask everyone to cast a vote (by putting a marker dot against specific skill perhaps) that they believe the Team should concentrate on as developing next. This part would resemble classing voting on Actions that usually come up at the end of a Scrum Retrospective, so should be familiar to you and those team members who have been exposed to properly set up Scrum process before.

Further part of this workshop could be up to you and the team, meaning that there could be desire to have further collaborative discussion and brainstorm on how to pair up for improvement of some development practices that are lacking perhaps, or who could run a brown bag session for the Team to lift overall understanding of a certain matter.

You as a Coach could gain invaluable insight into Team dynamics, levels of trust between the colleagues, overall proficiency levels, helping you form your own plan for what Coaching methods and Tools you could utilize next for the most impactful result.

Facilitate Sprint Planning

While this seems straightforward, I'd like to use this chance to emphasize importance of kicking off Agile/Scrum Practice clean-up with facilitating Sprint Planning for all Delivery Teams that you'll be looking after as Agile Coach.

This is your chance to hit several birds with one stone - taking a closer look at the health of Product Backlog that nominated Product Owner is considering to present to the Teams as part of planning, ensuring basic roles and responsibilities are understood from the just finished Fundamentals Training, as well as showing the Team the ropes of how Sprint planning should be done properly.

Teams might already have allocated Scrum Masters, who might even be perfectly capable performing setup of these basic events and Scrum process. This is perfectly fine, and you are not there to disrupt that process, and not to "audit" anyone's work. Try and make an effort so that everyone understands that your goals and purpose are different.

If you have an understanding with the Team's Scrum Master (or if they don't even have one yet), your job here is much simpler, as you come in to introduce the right practices and remind the Team about the theory they've just brushed up on during Fundamentals Training.

Even established Teams that might have already tried self-organization around Scrum roles and events usually benefit from a "guest" figure appearing to reinforce some elements of Scrum Framework that in 9 out of 10 cases get washed away by the reality of Teams returning into their familiar environment from the classroom, and having no Trainer watching them as they perform a certain recommended Event.

Agile Coach comes in here with a broader view of supporting Agile structures that usually allow to shed extra light on relatively black and white Scrum-prescribed way of doing things, enabling further learning process in Team members, and simply shaking things up for them a little bit.

It is important to be emotionally intelligent when approaching these events as they would almost always be seen as that "expert inspection" or audit of sorts, and what you want is to avoid that effect as much as possible, letting Scrum Master call the shots if they want or have to. Taking a step back, fading into the background when the Team tries to self-organize on top of something that doesn't require immediate correction is a good idea, as it shows initiative and - as we'll mention again in further chapters - it is okay to let the Team make mistakes.

A few of my colleagues have actually opted into simply observing how the Teams kick-off Scrum rituals based on their Fundamentals learnings, letting them run for a Sprint or two before intervening.

Their view upon this subject comes from the final note I made in the section above - that self-organization and letting Teams make mistakes is key in establishing proper learning culture, rather than holding their hand all the time, like a Trainer would do.

While I agree with this sentiment too, I still believe that the basic breakdown of coaching process, summarized as:

1. SHOW them how to do it properly,
2. LET THEM DO IT and learn from mistakes as they go,
3. SEE THEM TEACH OTHERS

Would work much better than the alternative:

1. LET THEM TRY AND LIKELY FAIL straight away,
2. SHOW them how to do it properly,
3. LET THEM DO IT and likely make mistakes anyway,

4. SEE THEM TEACH OTHERS, eventually.

Clean Up Scrum Practice Further

As mentioned above, and to expand upon the point of kicking off Scrum Practice with facilitation of a Sprint Planning, this is where you'd likely want to clean up the rest of Scrum Practice further.

Ensure all Roles are understood and filled. Discuss it with Teams and supporting Leadership if this isn't the case.

While risks of having no Tester (or Testing specialist, who would be co-located with each Delivery Team with the purpose of cross-skilling the other Developers, making the environment more cross-functional as the time goes on) could just be dealt with by being recorded and called out early on, this is hardly the right set-up for the Teams for success.

Same goes with a dedicated Product Owner. I found it being the most common challenge in Agile Transformations where new Delivery Teams are being thrown together, as Business won't nominate a Product Owner, or the nominated person simply wouldn't have enough time to do their new job properly.

This goes back to the chapter of being set up for success as a Coach, and as Delivery Teams that are supposed to embrace new ways of working and supply Customer Value. As a Coach you will have to repeat yourself many times, at different levels of your organization, being not just an educator but also an advocate for the right set-up being in place before anyone could start playing this new game seriously.

Among other things, ensuring that Sprint Retrospectives are not ignored and are happening properly is of paramount importance as the initial and most basic building block of a Continuous Improvement culture.

As a Coach you might have to reinforce the meaning of Retrospectives and ensure that they are also conducted properly, not necessarily in a classic boring way - but admittedly your Teams have to start somewhere.

Assist with Product Backlog Refinement

I've mentioned this as a potential earlier step in your Agile Coaching practice kick-off across the Teams, but wanted to emphasize the importance of setting this as a separate check-box for yourself when making sure the Transformation is off to a good start.

Review of the Product Backlog, and assisting the newly nominated "Product Team" with optimal ways of breaking down the incoming work into sizable chunks is something that could be done as a distinct separate step before you proceed to others.

Alternatively - and more commonly - it's being seen as a parallel activity that could overlap with the other things you'd be doing as a Coach during this initial phase, to make better use of time and allow Teams reach their "Scrum-readiness" earlier.

Your new Program of work or the Organization as a whole should have nominated some people from the Business side to step into the shoes of Product Owners, and in cases where larger scale of operations is realized immediately - even Product Managers.

If overall Agile maturity of the organization is not high enough yet - which would be a likely scenario given hypotheses we've assumed at the start of this book - you as a Coach would do well to run a "Product workshop", if not qualified to run a proper Product Owners Training.

Whether we like it or not, successful performance of certain duties starts with how well does an individual understand their role, and what they should be focusing on. That is certainly underpinned by personal motivation, which is a more complex topic that we'll discuss in a later chapter.

For now we'll assume that all of our nominees for new Agile roles are "ready and willing", otherwise the side-step and digression I'd have to take as part of this chapter would take us too far off topic…

Having been through Agile Fundamentals course with your Teams, including these Product Owners and Managers, presumably, you'll need to give them explanation that goes beyond those basics. Clarify for them that Product Owner is an inward-facing "Content Authority", co-located with the Team, while Product Manager is outward-facing, co-located with Business.

Product Manager identifies Market and Business opportunities for further prioritization of Product Features to deliver maximum Customer Value, while Product Owners translate that Vision and identified high-level Features into variably sized pieces of work, defined as clearly as possible for the Delivery Teams to estimate the work effort on.

We will assume that your organization will adopt standard Agile work breakdown structure, where we usually see Epics at the highest level, possibly stretching Releases of Product, Features being smaller pieces of work usually fitting into one Release, and User Stories and Tasks being smallest meaningful pieces complying with INVEST Model as much as possible.

In that case Product Manager owns the overall Product Roadmap, Vision, Program-level Backlog, and identifies Epic-level acceptance criteria. While Product Owner would own Team Product Backlog, define and priorities User Stories and determine Story-level acceptance criteria.

There's certainly more that could be said here, but this book doesn't focus on Product Owner training, and aims to just give you sufficient knowledge to start off with, and research further if required given your specific circumstances and needs.

When Product roles are well understood and enabled, you go into the specifics of work breakdown, probing some of those nominated Epics, Features and Stories, taking a look at their size, presence of acceptance criteria, testability, and other key criteria to writing good User Stories.

Make sure general directive of Product Backlog needing to contain literally everything that would need to be done during lifecycle of Product Delivery before it's in the hands of the Customer, including Non-Functional Requirements.

This could be a good time to also request the Teams to produce the initial version of their Definition of Done, as that would fit nicely into realization of what's the key difference between those all-applicable bullet-points, and the Acceptance Criteria for each individual User Story.

Remember that you are there to reinforce Agile Fundamental learnings that have been given the teams to set them off on their journey. Without repetition and someone holding their hand, especially early on, the likelihood of the Teams straying off course immediately is very high.

As mentioned above, some Coaches would just let teams fail and try and find their own way out of the ditch they've ended up with - perhaps with some help from the Coach - while I personally recommend additional hand-holding early on, to gain positive momentum as early as possible, letting Teams explore and make mistakes once that initial proper vector is established.

7 COACHING FRAMEWORK – PROGRESSING

So things are off to a good start, with you as new Agile Coach establishing core Agile practices, leading by example in terms of Values of transparency and collaboration.

The Teams should have adopted Scrum pretty well, progressing through their first few Sprints, learning to break down work better, estimate more accurately, and develop new habits of keeping Business involved and informed, rather than hiding any "bad news" from them.

All of relevant Leadership people have been Agile-trained, and you hopefully either conducted or got an approval from above to have your Product Owners properly trained as specialists in what remains one of the key elements of success - breaking down work, prioritizing well, and working with the Teams as collaboratively and positively as possible.

If you look back at Agile Coaching Journey diagram that I've presented to you in the earlier chapter, this virtual moment in time would be somewhere within "Basics" phase, around the line separating sub-phases of "Starting" and "Going/Progressing", probably leaning towards the second half a bit.

This is usually the time for you to "turn it up a notch", as they say, and start looking at 2nd priority activities and methods, that I'll summarize for you from my perspective in this chapter.

Before we dive deeper in, I'll just point out the obvious once again - the activities and tools suggested below do not absolutely have to wait for this sub-phase to begin before you introduce them to the Teams and other stakeholders.

As I mentioned multiple times, Coaching Journey is an individual undertaking, often directed and adjusted by large variety of factors, already established practices, culture of the company you are working for, and specific needs of the organization that should have been communicated to you when you're started in your role.

I've simply taken my own slice at the things that should be important to you as a Coach, and proposed order of activities that you could take those in. Regardless of how good you are, you can't do everything at the same time - why don't we follow classic Kanban Work In Progress Limit concept ourselves, since we'll be teaching it to the others soon enough, right?

Put simply, previous chapter contained items that I've prioritized as absolute level one for your Agile Coaching Journey kick-off. This chapter does what it says on the box - turns attention to what I believe is secondary compared to what we've covered before. It doesn't make the following activities any less important, *it just means that in my opinion, they could wait until now.*

Revisit Definition of Done, Help Refine It

As you should have established basic "5 minutes introduction" to what a Sprint-level Definition of Done is with the teams shortly following Scrum practice kick-off, now would be the time to encourage revision of those DoDs.

This is where you would re-emphasize to the teams the fact that Definitions of Done could be of multiple levels (unless you've covered this earlier), and that DoDs should evolve, as Team's understanding of their Scrum-based delivery practice evolves and matures.

Highlight once again that when something is marked "Done", it should be really done, finished. Not the common case of *"It's done, but needs to be re-tested and integration with other components hasn't been done…"* That's not "Done", and there are no other ways to honestly look at it - everything else falls under different forms of cheating.

This might also be the good time to reconcile Team-level Definitions of Done, to figure out similarities with the goal being to elevate that DoD to a Program Level, so that it starts applying to all delivery teams, without exceptions. This certainly requires higher maturity level of the development practice in place, and discipline of individual Team members.

Introduce Other Work Estimation Techniques

As your Agile Fundamentals training likely set your Teams off on their journey with bread and butter of Agile estimation process based on Fibonacci numbers sequence and the Planning Poker game, let's hope Teams have been practicing this basic estimation technique until now.

Assuming more work is pouring into the Product Backlog, creating solid base for further Sprints and Product Releases, there are other estimation techniques that you could start teaching your Teams and Product Owners.

Realistically, they all would benefit from learning about three core methods:

T-Shirt Sizing

Simplest yet practical estimation method of all, it still requires some explanation and baselining as far as practice goes, as you want to avoid confusion in understanding the rules.

1. Start by explaining that T-Shirt estimation is most commonly used for larger pieces of work (Epics and Features), when we don't know enough about the work itself - before anyone had a chance to dive into it, finding out every possible dependency and acceptance criteria.

2. Then allow the Team to discuss what would make sense as the T-Shirt Sizes Legend, i.e. what would your "S" stand for, and what would be an "L"? Actual conversion of sizes here could go as precise or as loose as your Teams and Leadership would deem necessary. It is important to understand that there should be some sense of relativity between all four sizes, where the higher the size is, the less confident you are in how accurate your estimation will be.

3. Make sure that estimation process involves all the relevant people, where review of Epics and Features happens with Business representatives, Product Owner, Technical Subject Matter Experts

(SMEs) from the Teams, Architects and possibly even Business Sponsor of the Program of work.

4. Typically you then go through the work items one by one, where Product Manager (who is normally responsible for Epic level of work) reads and explains those to the audience, giving them time to collaboratively discuss delivery options and ask questions to clarify Business requirements as necessary. Then the T-Shirt size is assigned, and Backlog record updated.

Planning Poker, Advanced Version

Classic gamified estimation technique, usually involving sets of cards with Fibonacci numbers on them - you should know this quite well, coming from anywhere within Agile Delivery, and having stepped into Agile Coaching shoes.

At this point in time (unless once again this was explained to them earlier) your Teams would most benefit from understanding that "shorthand versions" of Planning Poker work very well too, *without any cards*.

To prepare for this arguably a lot more practical method, you'll have to start by explaining to your Teams the "Fist of Five" technique:

1. Explain that normally Fist of Five technique is used to get a quick Vote of Confidence from a large audience of people, in regards to how certain they feel about a commitment to take on the amount of work in discussion, and deliver it successfully.

2. Prepare an image or a PowerPoint slide similar to the one above, display it in front of your Team(s) and ask them to give you vote of confidence that they'll read and understand the books displayed above. 1 finger means very little (or none at all) confidence, while 5 means - full confidence that they'll be able to complete the task. You should get full range of results, and quite a lot of fun out of it.

3. Highlight that it's not the only application of this really practical method that one could think of. This could be a great Team bonding opportunity and exercise you as a Coach should always look for an extra chance to introduce seamlessly, without disrupting general flow of whatever else your Teams were engaged in.

Once Fist of Five is understood and practiced, return audience's focus back to the topic of estimating work - this time User Stories, not the larger pieces like Epics or Features.

Explain to the Team that they'll be using Fist of Five to display their Fibonacci sequence number, closest to how many Story Points they'd be willing to give that particular User Story. They can use both hands if a Story is larger than 5 points, naturally.

As there is no such Fibonacci number as 10, and conveniently nobody is expected to have 13 fingers to display in case of a really large User Story, this method assumes that if a Team member voted showing 10 fingers, a quick round of clarification discussion will follow the vote, which usually takes only a few seconds.

When breaking down work to fit into an average Sprint, we discourage Story sizes larger than 13, so a vote of 10 fingers should draw attention of the Team and the Product Owner, possibly requiring further clarification of Story requirements, or maybe even a split of the Story into 2 or more.

Silent Triangulation, aka "Magic Estimation"

I almost guarantee that this rather simple yet uncommon method would be a breeze of fresh air for both your Teams and possibly even yourself, as a Coach only beginning your career outside of the routine cycle of Agile Delivery duties and core Scrum.

Silent Triangulation is often referred to as Magic Estimation, as this name is easier to remember, and the results can be - well - quite magical, given how quickly your Team could churn through a large number of Stories, reaching at least a broad preliminary agreement on their sizes.

Again, it's important to understand that the right tools have to be selected for the right job. In this case the method would work very well for smaller pieces of work (User Stories, Tasks) that are based on a known body of professional knowledge, e.g. further enhancements to the Product that the Team has been working on for a while, no majorly new or puzzling components.

In order for the exercise and method to work, it is assumed that Team members are familiar with subject matter to a reasonable extent, where they could make their own judgment of delivery effort without consulting with others. Making their decisions will be largely based on the obtained experience with the Product and delivery methods, and well phrased User Story itself - that should be clearly written on Story Cards you will use for the exercise.

Here is how I suggest to run the exercise:

Prepare a large surface to display your User Story cards or Tasks. This could be a Wall, or a large desk, which is a little less desirable as having cards horizontally might reduce their visibility for all the participants and observers.

Mark the columns of your grid - Backlog (*where you'll put all your User Story cards initially*), followed by each number of Fibonacci sequence that you are willing to allow your User Story sizing to stretch up to.

Something like this will do:

Backlog	1	2	3	5	8	13

Explain to the Team the simple rules - you will set a timer for 2 minutes, and each Team member should go up to the Wall and silently move any card into the column representing the right size/effort in their opinion. There shouldn't be any discussion or arguing, even if someone just moved "your" card from column "3" where you put it into column "8".

Backlog	1	2	3	5	8	13

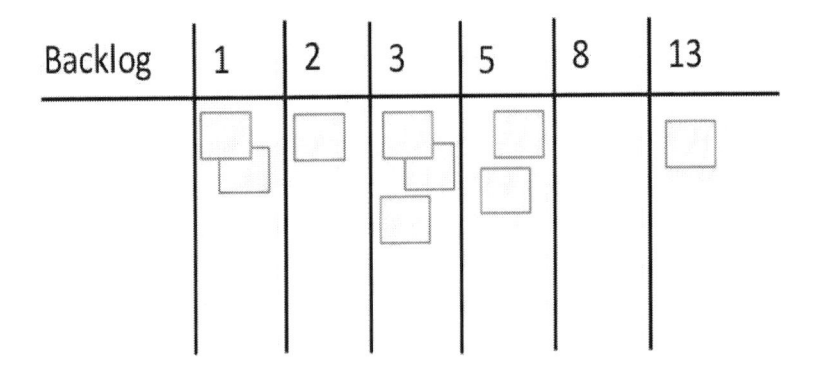

All discussion of discrepancies should be saved for after the initial shuffling has finished. Scrum Master (or an Agile Coach, if you are running this) should be the time-keeper and take note of any major discrepancies to bring to Team's attention after the exercise and discuss collaboratively. E.g. if something was moved from "2" to "13" there has to be some misunderstanding of requirements, acceptance criteria, or the other Team member simply doesn't know something.

In essence, as chaotic as this method sounds, in majority of cases it ends up in 80% accuracy of estimation for sometimes very large number of User Stories within those 2-3 minutes, plus relatively short follow-up discussion of discrepancies.

Introduce Agile Scaling Concepts

Again, depending on the needs of your organization, size of the Program of work undergoing Agile Transformation, and your individual goals as an Agile Coach, this could be the right time to start introducing Scaling concepts to the Teams and Leadership.

You should have been researching and speaking with the Leadership of this organizational Transformation about what they know about available methods to scale up Agile Delivery you've been helping them establish up to that point in time.

It's almost always beneficial to prepare a little presentation and a brown-bag session for broader audience, where you could explain and articulate pros and cons of different scaling methods, starting with natural cross-team coordination with standard Scrum delivery and synchronized cadence of Releases, and finishing with full-blown frameworks such as Scaled Agile Framework and Large-Scale Scrum.

Trying to list exact bullet-points highlighting benefits and negatives of each of those frameworks would be way beyond the scope of this book, that's supposed to set you off on the right track as Agile Coach - giving you direction for further research and self-development. This could be one of those opportune moments, if your current knowledge of the available frameworks is lacking.

Once you've grasped the main concepts of those frameworks and researched enough to be able to translate and articulate when the use of such a heavier construct would be justified within your company, running those info-sessions should spark some interest and create grounds for further discussion and training.

When approaching less Agile-savvy Leadership of your organization with the topic of Agile Scaling, it would be wise to have not just options and general information about "what exists out there", but to have a preferred option in mind, based on the facts I trust you would have reviewed by now.

Beyond your initial pitch and information session, choice and later adoption of Scaling concepts or a particular Framework will require extra learning, evolution of Roles, and further cultural shift from majority of people you would have been working with so far.

Do not expect to send everyone to a well-documented Scaled Agile Framework website packed with confusing information, give them a week to digest and then announce your first Program Increment (PI) Planning session. This would likely give a heart attack not to just the majority of people within your Delivery Teams, but maybe even yourself in the form of a well-deserved lash back.

There are a few prominent Agile Scaling frameworks out there at the time of writing this book, and I admittedly can't call myself an expert in all of those, to give them a fair and conclusive assessment here.

So instead I'll suggest one that I'm most familiar with, and that happens to be a very popular and almost "default" choice within the landscape of corporate Agile transformations in Australia - Scaled Agile Framework, abbreviated as SAFe.

As I mentioned above, it's not the aim of this book to give you full rundown of how SAFe works - that requires a different professional focus and qualification to mine, and also risks that I wouldn't give the framework all the justice it deserves.

So instead I'll give you a few quick bullet points of questions to ask yourself and your Leadership when considering if SAFe is suitable for your organization:

Are there more than 5 Delivery Teams assembled in accordance with Scrum Framework?

Are there more than 50 people in total, actively trying to collaborate and work out dependencies between themselves?

Is something consistently not working in meeting Business deadlines, expectations, and ensuring everyone is on the same page in terms of what's being agreed to be delivered, why, and by when?

If you've answered yes to all of the above, then SAFe could be a good Scaling Framework of choice for you. If not, you'd do well to research more alternatives, such as Large-Scale Scrum, or Scrum At Scale, which should give you a good number of results to read through if you ran a Google search for those terms.

Review Agile Walls

Accessibility, transparency and timeliness of information reflected on Agile Walls (sometimes being referred to as "Boards") cannot be overstated. As the Teams have surely set up their own Walls to reflect Sprint progress, by now you would have given them enough time to get into their own rhythm of updating those regularly.

I suggest a review pass over the Walls at this stage, to remind the Teams about the importance of keeping their houses neat and tidy, as informational hygiene is part of what makes Agile delivery appealing when it's done right, and maintained well.

Ever heard people say something about judging a book by its cover? Well, it's perfectly applicable in this case, as why shouldn't it be? Your "book cover" is what people see first, and that's your main Information Radiator - the Agile Wall.

If it's messy, out of date, or is maintained only for show, rather than as a useful tool to gather your thoughts around and have a collaborative discussion once in a while - all of this isn't pointing at a healthy Agile practice.

Which means you as a Coach have a lot more to do in that area...

These days many companies opt into bypassing physical Agile Walls, going straight for one of the numerous Agile Team collaboration tools, such as Atlassian JIRA, Trello, RTC, and many others.

I'm personally all for efficiency and elimination of wasteful processes and efforts, seeing benefit in working around digital Walls, especially if you have remote Scrum Teams being utilized as part of your Digital Delivery, such as Software Development.

Physical presence (or projection) of that Digital Wall in the Team space, where majority of people are presumably co-located is very important factor as well, which should be achieved if it's at all possible.

Inexpensive LED projector that the company could buy online for under $100 these days could do the trick, connected to a computer on corporate network and using that projector as a second monitor, reflecting your Team's Agile Wall onto virtually any flat surface. Lighting could be a consideration here, as good projectors that produce a good picture in broad daylight could actually be pretty expensive, but I'll leave technicalities up to you and your technical support people. Where there's Will, there's a Way!

Some of my Teams had simply a large TV screen connected to a computer and the Wall was displayed on it all day long, with updates being made as required, with Team members having access to the terminal.

The main couple of points I'm trying to make above are:

1. Team Agile Wall has to be used, maintained well, and evolve as required;

2. Even if Digital Wall is what's being used for everyone's benefit, there should be some sort of physical projection into Team's space, for both the onshore Team members, and the Leadership passing by.

Your job as a Coach is to emphasize the importance of those Walls to the Team and other stakeholders, encouraging feedback from Business in terms of whether or not they get meaningful information when coming around and taking a look at the Wall. Does it make sense to them? Can they tell how much work is being planned for the current Sprint and how well is the Team doing so far?

Feedback from Business or Leadership that decided to go on a *Gemba Walk*, visiting Delivery Team areas (which is one of the great Lean practices I advocate for) and observing such an Agile Wall could be invaluable for planning further exercises and activities with the Teams, as well as recognition of their success.

Revisit Quality of Sprint Reviews and Retrospectives

While this is part of core Scrum Practice that you would have established and continuously monitored through the initial part of beginning phase of your company's Agile Coaching and Transformation Journey, approaching Adoption Maturity phase is usually a good time to revisit such elements as Sprint Reviews and Retrospectives.

Even in well-oiled Delivery Systems there is a tendency to focus on the cogs that are actively turning, rather than supporting a perhaps less evident background structure, if you forgive the metaphor I'm using here…

In other words, Teams that haven't embraced Agile mindset fully yet, and are only showing good results sticking to the prescribed routines and Agile methods, would inevitably show some element of regression, where focus of their valuable time will shift into Planning of work and day-to-day execution duties.

With all luck, Sprint Reviews will also not be forgotten, as long as Business stakeholders remain engaged beyond the "novelty effect" that will wear off after a while as well. As Agile Coach dealing with interpersonal relationships and Team dynamics you should be aware of those tendencies, as this knowledge lies well beyond standard Agile/Scrum practice.

Team Retrospectives however might be seen as "too long", or Teams didn't notice as they've started assembling too many Action Items at the end of each Retrospective, resulting in a Backlog of those Action Items that realistically will never be fully actioned, and will require further prioritization beyond context of the relevant Retrospective itself.

You as a Coach should aim to check for presence of these regressive tendencies, and seek an opportunity to positively reinforce the meaning and importance of those elements of a Scrum cycle.

Specifically I would suggest that you checked and focused on fixing any of the following that produces negative result upon closer inspection:

1. How regularly are the Sprint Reviews happening? Are they skipping Sprints? As they should not be.

2. Is the Product Owner always present, and are they inviting some other key Business Stakeholders into those Review sessions?

3. Are the sessions running like a "Demo", where Teams are just showing what they've done, not seeking any particular feedback from the audience?

4. Are Retrospectives happening regularly as well?

5. Is Management "inviting themselves" into Retrospectives? If so, do you see any effects of Team members suppressing their honest feedback because Management is present?

6. How many Action Items is the Team producing per average Retrospective?

7. Is there Action Items prioritization element of Retrospective in place? How many do they shortlist to actually act upon at the end of the Retrospective?

8. What happens to the rest of Action Items that were put on the Retro Board, but didn't get enough votes on? Some teams create Backlog of those, which I recommend against. I would suggest only keeping those that Team is confident could be resolved or positively escalated as Actionable Items, and discard the rest. Those could be brought up during the next Retrospective if the problem persists - this is also likely to give those items more Team votes.

8 AGILE ADOPTION MATURITY

Maturity of Agile Adoption is one of those difficult things to pin down and define in a very specific manner, as it is assumed to be a phase of your transformation beyond learning new Agile methods, practices and making sure the teams developed habits to keep using those new ways of working for the foreseeable future.

Instead, it is the time when majority of your transforming organization and the key players driving this transformation have embraced the Agile mindset. It is when your Teams and Leadership stopped just *"doing Agile"*, they *"became Agile"*.

Their judgment calls, actions, planning, ways they cooperate with one another are now driven by Agile values and the mindset first and foremost, not rigorous following of some prescribed 1-2-3 steps an Agile framework you taught them to follow.

I've created the following diagram for one of my training sessions, which will help us pinpoint our location within the context of organizational transformation:

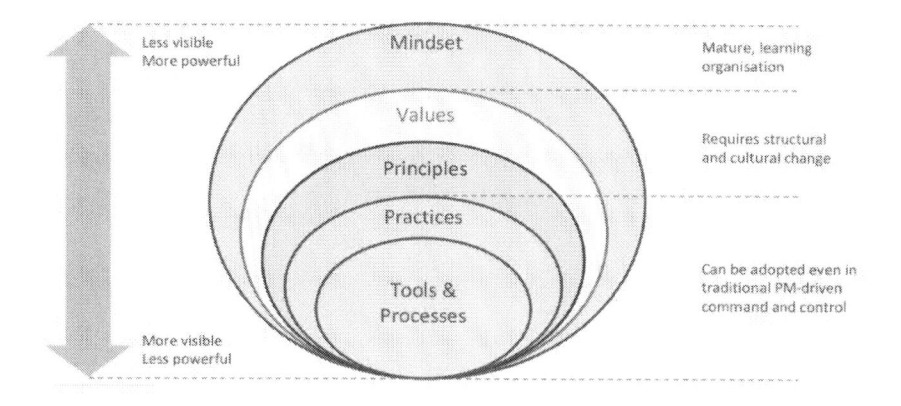

Diagram: Nested ovals from outer to inner — Mindset, Values, Principles, Practices, Tools & Processes. Left-side vertical arrow: top "Less visible / More powerful", bottom "More visible / Less powerful". Right-side labels: "Mature, learning organisation"; "Requires structural and cultural change"; "Can be adopted even in traditional PM-driven command and control".

Designed to be quite self-explanatory, it should be clear that your organization would have started its transformation journey from the Basics - Tools, Processes, Practices, then progressing to better embracing Principles and hopefully Values.

We naturally start with more visible items that deliver results quicker and help put our audiences into the right frame of mind, before they are able to start noticing how certain Agile principle or set of values start governing their actions and seemingly common sense-based decisions.

Actual start of this "Maturity" phase could be anywhere from 12 months into your organizational transformation, if all the factors are aligning in your favor as the spear-heading Agile Coach.

When that time comes, your day-to-day involvement as a full-time Agile Coach is likely to drop. That's what my earlier Coaching Journey diagram was displaying. You will have local champions enabled and willing to carry the flag of Agile in their daily activities, and your Teams would be cross-functional and mature enough to run their own show, most of the time.

You should be seeing consistent display of Teams embracing variety of learnings from what you (and possibly other Coaches on the ground already) taught them, as well as their own discoveries - results of their inspection and adaptation to the optimal mode of operation for themselves, fitting into your organization.

During this Agile Adoption Maturity phase you are likely going to become more of an observer and "on call" Service Provider, that Teams should be encouraged to reach out to when they need you, not expecting active day-to-day participation and 100% presence in their Team space.

Another important thing to understand here is that your starting point - the departure on this journey of coaching variety of people as part of their organizational transformation was relatively clear and easy for us to envisage, and for me to provide some specific guidance on.

There's the expected flow of typical Coaching Journey, common goals to see your people embrace new mindset and start showing sufficient maturity up to the level of them starting to teach and mentor others.

Then there are "Tools" that we've discussed - teaching actual helpful Agile practices and methods that would set your people off on the journey, mentoring them one-on-one where required, and basically responding to the needs of your particular company, that are likely going to be different from some other one.

As the time goes by however, and you are 6-12 months into the transformation, it is hard for an external advisor such as myself to predict what exactly you'd need to do and what tools from your Toolbox or Agile Coaching Framework would become relevant to you then.

You would know as a fellow Agile professional that we never plan beyond the horizon. Instead we always work with the best information at hand, laying out significant milestones, and doing more or less detailed planning only for foreseeable work that we could place some solid bets on.

Agile Coaching process is similar in that way, if you've been laying the right foundation, and using the elements we've discussed in the previous chapters. Plus my hope here is that you've been using advice from this book for what it was worth - making sure you understand the outline of a typical Coaching Journey, and what you could be doing as a Coach from day one.

Towards day 365, or whatever it would be in your case, when you start seeing that positive display of Agile Adoption across your Teams and Leadership - *you'll have to make a call on what your next step or milestone should be.*

It could be full-blown implementation of Scaled Agile Framework, with approved training for the whole organization performed externally by professional SAFe Trainers, including your own skills uplift as a Coach who might not have been officially trained and certified in SAFe.

Or it could be something completely different, such as "horizontal" expansion versus the default expectation of the need to expand "vertically", creating extra scaled-up layers within your Digital Delivery of Customer Value.

You could be put in charge of introducing similar Agile foundations and culture in some other part of your company that was just acquired by Business and needs to be brought on board. Or perhaps your Leadership and Agile Community of Practice (which I trust you would have established by this point!) decide against any bulky Scaled Frameworks, and decide to keep going with core Scrum, expanding towards Lean Thinking and more mature understanding of Kanban.

What I'm trying to say here is that your journey to this point should have created solid foundation for the people of your organization as well as yourself to make an educated further decision on what your major milestone for Agile Adoption Maturity phase should be.

Arguably there always should be one, as there's a law in physics that's saying that unless you set goals and keep moving forward, regression will take hold and you'll start moving backwards. Inertia is known not just to us as individuals, but also to organizations and specific Teams that are left to their own devices for too long.

Hence the observer and "on call Coach" role that yours would likely transform into at this stage.

Having said all of the above, in the spirit of the rest of this book, I'll list a few points that could be worth exploring as Agile Coach during this virtual Maturity of Agile Adoption phase.

As always, these are lead-ins into further research that I encourage you to invest your time into, if you feel like that particular point is applicable to your company and overall culture would benefit from it.

1. Does your Company or Program Leadership have a clear Vision, something that concisely defines Product strategy at high level moving forward? Defining that Vision and communicating it transparently to the Teams has a lot of benefits.

2. Is there a Value Stream concept in place? Something prominently featured as part of setting up Scaled Agile Framework, definition of those series of steps that deliver Customer Value, transparently visualizing it for everyone to see helps your Teams plan their work better, collaborating at scale even without the need to formally adopt a new framework.

3. Does your organization have someone properly understanding and being able to teach others the concepts of Design and Systems Thinking? Primarily relevant to the "problem-solvers" and those who plan the pipeline of work for the rest of Delivery Teams - Product Managers and Owners - these concepts are well worth introducing as early as necessary, and most definitely as one of the early elements of entering Agile Adoption Maturity phase.

4. Even without Scaled Agile Framework formally in place, there are

some techniques originating from it that could benefit your Product Team in planning their pipeline of high-level funded Initiatives and Features better. For example, you could look into work prioritization technique known as **Weighted Shortest Job First**, or **WSJF**.

This is certainly not an exhaustive list of everything you could try and put to good use as Agile Coach during the times when your Teams and Leadership are past Agile fundamentals and basics.

Life and work of an Agile Coach is in constant learning - about the people they work with and themselves - and this process usually naturally results in you discovering new and relevant pieces of knowledge you'd want to re-broadcast and share with your company.

In the next chapter we will talk about Agile Adoption Metrics in their basic form, that would allow you to delegate ownership of professional self-development to the Team members, as well as gauge how well the Teams are doing in their day-to-day use of Agile methods and practices you've been teaching them.

9 MEASURING AGILE ADOPTION

Before we talk about measuring Agile adoption, what are Skill adoption metrics, in general?

They are usually custom implementations of measurement of a predetermined skill or set of skills against a transparently displayed and easy to understand scaling system, or axis. Basically, it's a system that helps measure how proficient is a person or a Team of professionals at utilizing certain knowledge, methods or skills in their day-to-day duties.

Agile Adoption Metrics are similar systems of gauging levels of adoption of certain practices, and are themed around core skills and behaviors that an individual or a Team are supposed to be displaying as part of becoming more Agile.

As a reminder here - we don't generally "do" Agile, we "become" Agile as we embrace the values, principles and methods of collaborative work and incremental, transparent delivery of Value to the hypothetical Customer.

Are those metrics technically a type of reporting then? Yes and no.

As Agile professionals and Teams we aim to be transparent about our progress towards the goals we set, and about other elements of our health as a Community of Practitioners - risks we identify and capture, time we've been in the current cycle of Value delivery, and other things.

This could include Team skill and Agile adoption levels as well.

So who do those Metrics help, and why? Multiple layers of involved stakeholders, Leadership of organizational transformation, as well as the Team members.

It's only logical that the organization deciding to undergo an Agile transformation as a whole or in part would like to have a method of tracking how it's generally traveling in the right direction.

Adoption of a new culture and embracing certain skills and behaviors is not something that can be necessarily timed, or rushed to - provided you want to establish a long-lasting learning and continuous improvement culture. But as an Agile Coach you would still inevitably draw a timeline indicating major milestones that you'd track your progress by.

For example, you could set the goal for yourself to roll out Fundamentals training across the whole organization within the first month from the transformation kick-off. Then you set another virtual milestone for yourself to make sure Scrum practice is solidly in place within the next two months, and so on. All of this will obviously depend on the size of your organization and your individual remit as a single Agile Coach, looking after given number of Teams and people.

So how do you implement a basic Agile Adoption Metrics system, and what should it look like? Let's go through the main steps I recommend, until you feel confident enough to make adjustments to this plan and tweak it the way you see fit.

1- Identify key Agile practices

Being an Agile Coach, I trust you'd be able to produce an initial list of key Agile practices and methods you'd want the Teams to start embracing from the kick-off of the transformation.

Assuming you are not alone in this process, I'd recommend that you meet with your Agile Community of Practice - other Agile Coaches and Scrum Masters - or at the very least the Leadership of organizational Transformation to go through the list of those proposed key Agile practices, before circulating it to the Teams.

It's usually a good idea to treat your Delivery Teams and other involved stakeholders respectfully, like smart professionals, even if they aren't fully Agile yet - they could still provide you with valuable input if you asked them if they had anything to add to the list of practices and methods you've identified.

Perhaps an invitation to review the list and provide feedback by a certain date not too far away would also boost the buy-in of individuals into what you'd be asking them to do next.

2- Define a Legend, or Scale of Measurement

Just as important as agreement on the key metrics you'll be aiming to measure, you would need to collaboratively develop and agree the Legend that will transparently indicate adoption level for each and every method and practice you'll include in your system.

You want to make sure everyone understands exactly what each level of adoption means, and that there is no confusion. Speaking the same language is important, especially if your assessment process involves a step where it won't be facilitated by yourself in person - asking Team members to do something in their own time.

So as a starting example, you could propose measurement indicators for 4 key adoption levels:

1. No adoption whatsoever;
2. Practice or method in place, but desires a lot of improvement;
3. Practice or method in place, performed confidently and consistently;
4. Practice or method in place, Teams showing maturity of adoption, self-sufficient.

You might want to expand the above to show one or two more points, if you feel like that level of granularity will help the Teams and yourself with assessment.

3- Create the Dashboard

Next you'd create a simple Table-based Dashboard, similar to the screenshots I'm providing below, where you'd list all key practices you'd like to measure, and your columns would represent each of adoption levels.

Once you are happy with clarity of the template you've produced, circulate it to all Delivery Teams you'd like to request the initial self-assessment from. Always welcome feedback.

4- Request Self-Assessment, Explain the Rules

Then the Teams would be requested to conduct self-assessment against given key metrics. You as a Coach should explain the Rules, and usually leave it to Team's Scrum Masters to facilitate this quick exercise as part of their next Retrospective or Sprint Planning.

The Rules:

1. One printed out Metrics assessment template per Team, transparently displayed as part of the exercise. They could print the template out on an A4 (or A3 for better visibility) and hang it on the Wall, or just pass around the table.

2. Each Team member gets to place *one vote per listed key Agile practice*, method or skill, then passes the turn to the next Team member. They should be encouraged to express personal opinion on how they think their Team is doing to date in adoption of that specific practice, method or skill.

3. This is not a public vote exercise, and everyone is entitled to their own opinion. Team members should not have to explain why they scored certain Agile practice or method so high or low. The only adjustment and influence allowed here is for facilitating Scrum Master or Agile Coach to make sure everyone fully understands what the ideal scenario of embracing a certain Agile method entails. Such as - perhaps a quick reminder of how a proper Daily Scrum should run, or how a Sprint Planning should be conducted.

4. Once the exercise is finished, the marked template with Team scores is passed back to the Agile Coach for their own assessment.

Your Agile Adoption Metrics self-assessment template could look something like this, after the initial exercise is completed:

DRAGONS

TEAM'S SELF-ASSESSMENT

ADOPTION PRACTICE	★	★★	★★★	♛
TRAINING DONE		II	I	
AGILE WALL	I		II	
PRODUCT BACKLOG		I	II	
SPRINT PLANNING		II	I	
DAILY SCRUM			II	I
SPRINT REVIEWS	II	I		
RETROSPECTIVES		III		

5- Agile Coach does their own assessment

You as Team's Agile Coach, or perhaps as a whole Agile Community of Practice at that point would then do your own overlapping assessment of the Team's level of adoption of those key practices and methods.

This would create an opportunity to inspect how much range is there in your level of scoring versus how the Team is largely seeing themselves on the available scale. This is not about spotting "wrong" or unrealistic views of Team members, but to indicate further coaching opportunities - especially in the areas where you see a lot of votes landing very low.

Perhaps they've voted too conservatively, not scoring themselves high enough against something that you actually believe they've been doing as a Team quite well? Or maybe it's the opposite picture, where a lot of Team members feel like they are "self-sufficient" in how their Sprint Reviews are done, while you think there's much those still desire.

Regardless, of the actual result and conclusions, Agile Adoption Metrics system and self-assessment exercise is a fantastic tool to use at certain milestones of your establishment of a new working culture, allowing you to create or adjust your plan of what further teaching of 1 on 1 coaching might be beneficial in some areas.

After your Coaching assessment is done, the picture might look like this:

DRAGONS — COMBINED ASSESSMENT

ADOPTION PRACTICE	★	★★	★★★	♛
TRAINING DONE		III	I	
AGILE WALL	I	I	II	
PRODUCT BACKLOG		I	III	
SPRINT PLANNING		III	I	
DAILY SCRUM		I	II	I
SPRINT REVIEWS	III	I		
RETROSPECTIVES		III	I	

6- Review with the Team

It's almost always a good idea to review the results with the Team, face to face, during a friendly lunch session, or perhaps as part of another Retrospective.

This once again is not an "explain yourselves" session, but to share your Coaching observations that emerged from the exercise, proposing some further activities or sessions that the Team might welcome to make them feel more confident in the certain practice or method for the next similar checkpoint.

It is important to understand and explain to the Teams that these key identified Agile practices and methods you were measuring during phase while Basics were introduced to the teams will change, as their relevance changes between different phases of the coaching journey and Agile transformation as a whole.

So next time you do similar Agile Adoption assessment, your dashboard might change to include a new more relevant set of metrics, such as:

DRAGONS MATURITY PHASE — COMBINED ASSESSMENT

ADOPTION PRACTICE	★	★★	★★★	♛
SAFe® TRAINING		III	I	
PROGRAM KANBAN	I	I	II	
FEATURE QUALITY		I	III	
PI PLANNING		III	I	
INSPECT & ADAPT		I	II	I
SYSTEM DEMO	III	I		
INNOVATION		III	I	

Regardless of your actual approach to conducting these exercises, or which Agile practices and methods to include, such "soft measurement" of Teams process is a definitely useful tool that gives a lot of information to the individual Team members, as well as yourself as a coach.

10 COACHING DEFINITION OF DONE

Concept of Definition of Done for an Agile Coach is closely linked to the phase of Agile Transformation when your teams approach relative Maturity in adoption of Agile Mindset - Principles and Values that drive us, as well as Practices and Methods that serve as our Tools of the Trade.

Put simply, unlike a lot of Delivery or Management roles, a Coaching role could be "Done" - at least if we keep considering full-time coaching capacity.

Before you get too confused and start thinking of those commonly used analogies as there's always a Coach for any persistent sports Team, and their job is sort of never "Done", let me clarify that I talk about realities of an Agile Coach life within a corporate structure of transforming organization.

Part of what you do is create sustainable culture, role setup, knowledge levels, behavioral patterns that keep driving your people forward, creating that mature Agile learning mindset. In that environment analogy of a sports Coach suits more the roles that are permanently embedded with the Teams - for example Scrum Masters.

Let's not forget that Scrum Masters have some Agile Coaching responsibility, even though they approach it from the slightly limited perspective of Scrum Framework. But their real job is to teach the teams about Scrum and keep setting the pace for the Team, going forward, potentially indefinitely.

As we've discussed differences between Scrum Master and Agile Coach roles, among other things we've mentioned that Coach comes in to create learning culture and provide extra volume of knowledge necessary for that successful kick-off. Coach helps people become more Agile, *not just by doing stuff, but by being who they are* - radiators of Agility within an organization hiring them.

Going back to the realistic situation that's likely to happen within your organization, during the phase of achieved Agile Adoption Maturity, as well as ticking off a few specific checkboxes I'll list for you below, it is likely that a lot of Agile Transformation muscle that was built up heavily upfront will not be necessary to the same extent anymore.

From the perspective of Transformation Leadership of the organization, it's like delivering a Product to the Customer. In hypothetical situation where there's no further features in the roadmap for this "Product", all you'll need is a crew to support the Product going forward.

All the "heavy lifting" associated with building architectural base, skill-sets across Delivery Teams, processes related to development and release of your Product, and other elements would be already done.

You will struggle to find any official statements where some large company declared that their Agile Transformation is "Done" some 24 months after they've embarked on their own journey. They would likely show some results, report on some achievements and showcase how well their Teams are working these days, compared to when they were just starting, but you'll struggle to catch anyone conclusively stating - "We are Done!"

The "End" of an Agile Transformation when that Coaching Definition of Done gets filled with green ticks against multitude of things that need to be in place is a behind the scenes thing, usually, with no formal sign-offs involved. There could be an internal celebration to acknowledge several Releases made using newly adopted Agile Delivery methods and Culture - in fact I'd say there ought to be one! - but that's probably all you'll be able to dig out and experience.

But behind the scenes people keeping the hand on the pulse of the Transformation, monitoring releases of some Product to the Customer, trends within Business Key Performance Indicators, Customer Satisfaction Survey results, NPS, and other blinking lights on that imaginary dashboard, will notice that the heavy crew of specializing Agilists - such as Coaches - would no longer be required with the current numbers.

I have to keep clarifying here as dry text doesn't allow me to convey the full picture to you immediately, that I'm talking about typical situation that required a full-blown Agile Transformation in the first place - a medium to large corporate entity, or a large enough Program of work within a certain company of even larger scale.

Those are usually the ones hiring Agile Coaches on top of Agile Delivery Team members such as Product Owners and Scrum Masters in the first place.

And as I've mentioned in the chapter where we talked about setting yourself as a Coach up for success - you are unlikely to be able to do all of this alone. So by the time of this Maturity phase where Coaching Definition of Done even becomes a thing, there are very high chances that you'll have a number of Agile Coaches on the ground - not just yourself.

Hopefully the above, albeit wordy, starts giving you the right picture of the timing and situation within your company when you as individual Agile Coach, and your whole Agile Community of Practice should check your Definition of Done (DoD) for completion of those goals, that you've inadvertently or deliberately set for yourselves at some point.

So What Is a Coaching DoD?

Coaching Definition of Done is similar to your usual Scrum Team DoD that applies to individual pieces of work flowing through the Value Stream of your organization, getting marked as "Done".

It is a transparent list of points that your Agile Community of Practice and Transformation Leadership agreed on, and that encompass all the main Agile practices, methods, behaviors, Team compositions, reporting lines, particulars of interactions with the Teams and Business stakeholders that you expect to be seen across the transforming organization in order for you as a Coach to consider your job "Done".

As the sizable intro into this chapter suggested, the point in time when you'd seriously look through your Coaching DoD and start ticking things off is really up to you and your organization.

It rarely makes sense "chipping at it" - ticking off one item 3 months into the transformation, while the rest become incomplete or far from accomplished. You could certainly pencil in some ticks, as part of your Community of Practice meetings, but as the time passes, situation around those early ticks that you might have placed on your Coaching DoD could have changed.

In other words, proper review of your Definition of Done should happen as a vertical slice at some point in time when you have reasons to believe that your work might be complete, at a major scale, across the board. Then you'd check and audit every bit of your Practice, making sure Continuous Improvement culture of basic Retrospectives is not forgotten under months of trying to adopt more complex behaviors and practices of Scaled Agile Framework, for example.

Also as with any other standard Definition of Done, it has to be discussed and evolved by your Coaching Community of Practice and the Leadership. You can't just create a DoD for yourself as an Agile Coach in isolation, and try and measure completeness of your work across the board like that.

Basic Coaching Definition of Done

So here is what I'd put on the initial draft version of your Coaching Definition of Done that you could bring into the first meeting with your colleagues and Transformation Leadership, to discuss and evolve further.

We keep assuming large-scale organization with dozens of Delivery Teams involved that decided to go with implementation of a Scaled Agile Framework as one of their indicators of reaching Adoption Maturity phase.

If your scale of operation is smaller and no Scaled Agile Framework is in place as one of key End Goals, adjust the list below accordingly.

1 - Portfolio Layer is established

1.1 - All new roles required by the selected Framework are filled internally or via external recruitment process, availability and capacity of people performing those roles is not in question. *This is applicable to all Layers that are part of this DoD*;

1.2 - People are trained to perform those roles, and motivated personally. No one is visibly dragging their feet, or is identified as a solid detractor remaining part of the machine. *This is applicable to all Layers that are part of this DoD*;

1.3 - Portfolio Kanban is established and well maintained. There are clearly defined Value Streams, and transparently visualized flow of larger funded pieces of work (Epics) to delivery towards known Key Performance Indicators;

1.4 - Portfolio Backlog includes not just Functional Epics, but also Enabler Epics and Non Functional Requirements;

1.5 - Funding Model appropriate for incremental delivery of Customer Value is in place;

2 - Program Layer is established

2.1 - There are one or more Agile Release Trains in place, with all required roles filled and trained in SAFe;

2.2 - Program Increment Planning is happening, and Objectives are clearly set for the whole Train;

2.3 - At least three Program Increments have been successfully planned and delivered with increasing performance and involvement from all the required parties, as per SAFe training;

2.4 - Continuous Delivery Pipeline is established across the Train, with key Practices such as Continuous Integration, Continuous Deployment and Release on Demand;

2.5 - There is an Architectural Runway in place, that is maintained and owned properly;

2.6 - There is a solid aspiration across the teams and Train as whole towards DevOps culture, including such elements as Automation across the board, Lean Flow, Measurement, and Recovery Strategy;

2.7 - There are System Demos happening regularly at the end of the planned Program Increment, and all key stakeholders from Business and IT are keenly participating in those;

3 - Delivery Teams Layer is established

3.1 - All Delivery Teams are assembled, trained, and performing according to your expectations as Agile Coaching Practice. Agile Adoption Metrics assessment checkpoints should help measure and keep track of this element;

3.2 - Development and Release of Customer Value is happening on a synchronized cadence across the Agile Release Train that any particular Team is part of;

3.2 - Individual Team Agile Walls are set up and maintained in good quality;

3.3 - Fundamental Agile practices relevant to the delivery method or framework of choice (such as Scrum or Kanban) are solidly in place - all rituals are happening, roles are filled and performed well, Product Owners are present;

3.4 - Continuous Improvement culture now appears to be native to the organization as a whole, and individual Teams;

3.5 - Staff training plans are in place, with uplift of Teams skills happening as regularly as required.

This sample Coaching Definition of Done is far from complete, and I hope it's obvious to you as my reader this late in the book. Your journey is unique, as the needs of your whole organization.

It also should be pretty obvious that even just considering the sample points I've listed for you above, it doesn't look like a small and quick journey that would end for you quickly as a Coach investing their professional time and heart into it.

My goal here was to give you a taste and purpose that such DoD could serve, when you could either consider shifting your efforts towards some other part of Business you work for, that still does require a full-time Coaching resource, or side-shift your activities somewhere where you'd add more value.

11 CONCLUSION

And there you have it my friends, wrap-up point of this virtual Agile Coaching journey that I hope you've enjoyed and learned something from.

Before I let you go off into the world of infinite and usually subjective knowledge areas surrounding the whole matter of Agile Coaching practice, I'd like to recap what I believe are the main learning points one should have gotten out of all of this.

Becoming an Agile Coach is not for everyone.

While the title is becoming more and more popular on the job market, also usually paying more than other Agile Delivery roles such as Scrum Master, I would not call it a logical career progression step for anyone who's done their years helping Teams adopt Scrum and deliver Value better.

Agile Coaching requires not just skill and additional knowledge, but also a certain personality, personal goals, and sense of professional purpose.

Dedicating your professional career to optimization of Digital Delivery practices surrounding Scrum, focusing predominantly on one Team at a time, making sure they understand basics of Agile and how Scrum is supposed to work is very different from the purpose and the breadth of what an Agile

Coach is supposed to be looking after.

Specifics of the goals and remit that hiring company would place upon their Agile Coaches could be very different, but there is a typical direction most organizations take in their transformations - something you as a fresh Agile Coach have hopefully learned more about after reading this book.

Being an Agile Coach means being a teacher to multiple layers of your company's structure. While Scrum Masters would be your Agile champions that face predominantly inward - their Teams - you as Agile Coach would be the radiator of Agility floating in several areas of the organization, dealing with the Teams as much as you would with the Leadership and Business stakeholders.

Instilling the right culture, making sure Agile Values are well understood and start forming into a new Mindset across the organization is how I'd define your ultimate purpose as an Agile Coach.

Methods, frameworks, even practices change over time - sometimes radically. Some come into fashion, such as "Spotify Model" that so many professionals are fixated upon at the end of 2017, while others fade into the background and are claimed to be no longer cutting-edge. But Lean Agile Values and Mindset surrounding those is something a lot more consistent and underpinning whatever it is that we'll face as professionals over the coming years.

Investing into the growth of your knowledge and practical skills conducting coaching sessions, running trainings, speaking in front of large audiences of people, as well as keeping up with what's happening in the areas of Lean and Agile are habits that you should develop in yourself, if you've decided that teaching others be better is something that you'd like to be doing going forward.

While I still believe that any professional career is a journey, rather than a marriage, i.e. it's a lot more welcoming of pivots and changes in your direction and choices you've made at one point, knowing the matter that you are considering to invest yourself into will undoubtedly save you a lot of trouble, time and effort.

Further Reading and Education

As I mentioned in the little wrap-up chapter above, this book focused on Agile Coaching as a Journey, offering our new recruits some basic understanding and Tools to get the job done, while they develop their own expertise and preferred set of methods.

Your search for other Agile Coaching books on Amazon should give you a few more titles that have done a good job on diving deeper into the actual methods of coaching the Teams - something I felt would be redundant to repeat in my own words, but probably worth for you to inspecting and consider reading.

As further education, I'd like to offer you the following content:

My Podcast

I'd be delighted to welcome you as a new subscriber to my weekly **Lean and Mean Agile Podcast**, which takes the approach similar to this book - remaining rather informal yet hopefully informative and entertaining.

The podcast covers everything from Agile Fundamentals, to Coaching basics, Lean Thinking, and interviews with the real people from Agile professional space, offering their opinions on the key matters that you - listeners - are interested in.

On SoundCloud: https://soundcloud.com/user-364782318

On iTunes: https://itunes.apple.com/au/podcast/lean-and-mean-agile-podcast/id1269551866

Podcast feedback, questions and requests are welcome here - podcast@joinagile.com.

"Get Hired as Scrum Master" Book on Amazon

If you find yourself in a professional career development phase preceding the one realistically necessary to benefit from the learnings given in this Agile Coaching book, I have another one for you:

"Get Hired As Scrum Master" - https://www.amazon.com/GET-HIRED-SCRUM-MASTER-Transitioning-ebook/dp/B01I1OVEV0

It also addresses job applicants who have decided to take their very first steps towards Agile Project Management and Digital Delivery professional space, transitioning from other roles, and aspiring to become Scrum Masters.

We saw a lot of professionals change their jobs from Software Developers, Business Analysts, Project Managers, Technical Team Leaders and others to some form of Agile Delivery professionals such as Scrum Masters over the past few years.

I've been through this process myself, learning first-hand what works and what doesn't when it comes to breaching the "Wall of Recruiters" that usually stand between you and that job of a Scrum Master that you might desire. The influx of competing applicants is so large - *at least in Australian job market of 2016-2017* - that you'd be severely reducing your chances of being shortlisted for job interviews and getting hired if you are not trying to be ahead of the crowd.

Lack of specific knowledge about how Agile job market works, how to properly prepare yourself and your professional Resume, how to handle Agile interview questions appropriately, what specific knowledge and experience to build up is what would be holding you back.

Written primarily for aspiring professionals who want to enter the world of Agile Project Management and Digital Delivery, but who do not possess the right knowledge or insights yet, **"Get Hired As Scrum Master"** is my attempt to share my personal findings and summarize research made as part of becoming a Professional Scrum Master.

You'll read plenty of my subjective but educated opinions on a number of topics surrounding general theme of presenting yourself as the most appealing Agile job candidate, receiving advice on how to work with your current professional background, pivoting towards a Scrum Master within Agile Digital Delivery in the most efficient way.

Among other things the book will teach you:

- What requirements apply to Scrum Master role candidates these days;
- How to deal with Recruiters and get your application through their initial filter;
- How different companies see Scrum Master roles and responsibilities;
- What are Agile Hybrid roles, and why should it concern Scrum Masters;
- How to do your research and other preparation properly;
- How to write a good to-the-point Cover Letter, and do you need one at all;
- How to reformat your Resume and present it the best possible way;
- What interview questions a new Scrum Master can expect, and the best ways to respond.

Sounds like something you or your colleagues could benefit from?

Well, then feel free to buy me another coffee and grab the book from Amazon today.

Feedback

Your feedback, wishes for future editions of this book, are most welcome and should be sent to my email - hello@joinagile.com.

You could also connect to me on LinkedIn (https://www.linkedin.com/in/iarandine/) and Twitter (https://twitter.com/iarandine).

I will endeavor to respond to any constructive feedback I receive.

ABOUT THE AUTHOR

Dmitri Iarandine is a Lean Agile Coach, Professional Scrum Master, Podcaster and Speaker with over 15 years of combined experience in Agile Software Development, Delivery and Coaching across industries in Australia.

Believer in custom implementations of Agile practices responding to specific needs of any company, rather than one-size-fits-all classroom theory, Dmitri helped transform multiple organizations, improving productivity and building culture fit for modern competitive market.

Printed in Poland
by Amazon Fulfillment
Poland Sp. z o.o., Wrocław